Deduct Everything!

Save Money with Hundreds of Legal Tax Breaks, Credits, Write-Offs, and Loopholes

EVA ROSENBERG, EA

Humanix Books

Deduct Everything
Copyright © 2016 by Eva Rosenberg
All rights reserved

Humanix Books, P.O. Box 20989, West Palm Beach, FL 33416, USA
www.humanixbooks.com | info@humanixbooks.com

Library of Congress Cataloging-in-Publication Data

Names: Rosenberg, Eva, author.
Title: Deduct everything : save money with hundreds of legal tax breaks, cred-
    its, write-offs, and loopholes / Eva Rosenberg.
Description: Boca Raton, Florida : Humanix Books, 2016.
Identifiers: LCCN 2015047996 (print) | LCCN 2015049893 (ebook) |
    ISBN 9781630060473 (paperback) | ISBN 9781630060480 (Paperback)
Subjects: LCSH: Finance, Personal. | BISAC: BUSINESS & ECONOMICS /
    Personal Finance / Money Management. | BUSINESS & ECONOMICS /
    Small Business. |BUSINESS & ECONOMICS / Taxation / Small Business.
Classification: LCC HG179 .R674 2016 (print) | LCC HG179 (ebook) |
    DDC 343.7305/23—dc23
LC record available at http://lccn.loc.gov/2015047996

Interior Design: Scribe

Humanix Books is a division of Humanix Publishing, LLC. Its trademark, consisting of the words "Humanix" is registered in the Patent and Trademark Office and in other countries.

Disclaimer: The information presented in this book is meant to be used for general resource purposes only; it is not intended as specific financial advice for any individual and should not substitute financial advice from a finance professional.

ISBN: 978-1-63006-047-3 (Paperback)
ISBN: 978-1-63006-048-0 (E-book)

Printed in the United States of America
10 9 8 7 6 5 4 3 2

Contents

CHAPTER 1

Introduction

For more than a decade, I have been known as the "TaxMama®"—the "Dear Abby" of the tax world—fielding questions from Americans and visa holders the world over through my website, www.TaxMama.com. It's been a lot of fun. The questions people ask, the glimpses into people's lives, their ideas and perspectives are fascinating. I am privileged to be trusted with such intimate details. Some people have been part of TaxMama's family from the beginning. And some pitch in and help out, providing insights and tips from their own rich store of knowledge.

The fact is the Internal Revenue Code (IRC) is bloated. According to Nina Olson, your National Taxpayer Advocate, by 2012, the IRC had grown beyond four million words—more than double the size of the IRC in 2001. Imagine how much it's grown in the last three or four years! In fact, just as we were about to publish this book, Congress passed the "Protecting

Americans from Tax Hikes Act of 2015" on December 18, 2015. That gave us time to make notes about the last-minute changes before we went to press. See Bonus Tip #270 for more details.

Absolutely no one can be expected to know everything in the Tax Code. Not you, not your tax professional (or tax expert), not the IRS—no one. We've all heard the phrase, "Ignorance of the law is no excuse." So what's the secret to getting it right?

TaxMama's Secret is *R & R*—Reliable sources and Research. We know who to ask. We know where to look.

My goal is to teach you those two things: who to ask and where to look for accurate answers.

I want the tax process to be a fun experience for you, one that challenges you to use your wits to dream up your own ideas on how to "beat the system." Legally, of course! Sometimes your far-fetched ideas might actually turn out to be the perfect solution. (In fact, I won my Dow Jones column by trying to sell a far-fetched idea a reader had sent me—an idea that turned out to actually work! More about that in "A Few Last Words.")

Along the way, you'll get tips, ideas, and strategies that you can implement immediately.

We'll try to make the book as user friendly as possible, with a Resources section that will take you directly to the information you need.

First, I want to offer you my hard-won insights and truisms to help guide you throughout your tax journey.

TaxMama's Tax Truisms

Philosophy about taxes: Lower taxes, achieved ethically = higher profits and increased joy.

Mantra about tax return records: Document, document, document! In other words, get a backup for everything!

Philosophy about people in general: There's never a bad time to be nice to someone. There's never a bad time to say something nice to someone. In fact, say or write something nice to someone right now!

Philosophy about dealing with IRS and state officials: Always be gracious and polite to IRS, state, and other tax officials. They can either help you or do you great harm. While it's illegal to give gifts to government officials, you are welcome to write a letter of commendation to thank them for helping you. Send it to them with a copy for their superiors. These letters go into the employee's file and help with promotions, commendations, and other advancements. Besides, it always feels good to get a compliment.

Philosophy about getting even: What's the best way to get even with someone who is really mean and nasty? Smile and be super nice to them at all times. It will totally confound them.

Philosophy about burnout: Sometimes, even when you love doing something, too much of a good thing becomes a burden. Take a break.

Philosophy about tax filing when you think you have no taxable income: Always file a tax return whether you need to or not. Why? Because TaxMama said so. You never know what future trouble you will forestall. If you don't file, you will find out in about five years—and it will be hell. If you do file, you will never know the trouble you've missed.

Philosophy about not filing when you have refunds due: Never leave money on the table. Not filing because you have a refund coming and will collect it later is . . . how can I say this diplomatically? I can't. It's *stupid*! After three years, you lose your refund. I actually had a client who lost more than $100,000 because he didn't file his tax return for more than ten years and had five-figure refunds each year. It can happen to you, too!

Philosophy about caregivers who don't want to report their income: If a childcare facility is cheating on their taxes and lying to the IRS, do you really want them being your children's caregivers? If they refuse to provide a Social Security number to you, what will they teach your children about right and wrong?

Philosophy about someone who wants to work outside a system: If someone is ripping off their suppliers or marketers (like going around AirBnB's rules, or house cleaners who want you to hire them without their agency), can you trust them not to cheat you, too?

Philosophy about extending credit to someone who doesn't pay proper taxes: If someone has avoided paying the IRS for years, do you really think they will be afraid of your bill collections efforts?

Philosophy about finding treasure: Search the Unclaimed Money site at least once a year (https://www.usa.gov/unclaimed -money). You never know what treasures you will find. I found money for my cousin that had been left unclaimed by her deceased mother.

How to Use This Book

This book is designed to give you some tips you probably won't find anywhere else.

It isn't intended to regurgitate the tax laws and deductions that you already know and are, quite frankly, bored with.

I try not to use any acronyms in a chapter without explaining it in that chapter. Once explained in the chapter, I will probably use it relentlessly.

Except one.

AGI—you will see this one acronym throughout the book, used mercilessly. It is the heart of the entire income tax computation. It stands for Adjusted Gross Income. This is a specific amount that you will find at the bottom of page one of your long-form 1040. (The same number is found at the top of page two of the long-form 1040.)

Regardless, if you encounter a term or acronym that is unexplained, please turn to the Glossary at the back of the book. You will find all the explanations there.

Part of TaxMama's philosophy is, "If it's too good to be true, it probably isn't true."

So when I give you a tip or guidance that is too good to be believed, you will find a reference. In the print book, you will be given an IRS publication number, a code section, a Tax Court case, or some other useful reference. In the electronic version of the book, you will find links directly to that part of the publication or links directly to the specific source of the information.

You would be wise never to take advice on faith. Please look things up, research them. Learn how to read and understand what is happening in your tax life. After all, when you sign a tax return or other tax form, you are attesting that you have read it, understand it, and are responsible for the contents.

Naturally, researching, reading, and learning take a lot of time. That's what tax professionals do—often, because we think it's fun. But perhaps you are like Isaac Asimov. Remember him, the famous scientist and mathematician best known for having written more than five hundred books? He is known for his "Three Laws of Robotics," and many of his books have become films—including *I, Robot*, *Bicentennial Man*, and his chilling short story "Nightfall."

One April, he devoted an entire editorial column in *The Magazine of Fantasy & Science Fiction* to tax season. The Good Doctor, as Asimov was known, explained why he uses a tax professional: "I am sure I could understand income taxes if I put my mind to them. But if I took the time to do that, the world would be deprived of many of my books."

If a genius like Isaac Asimov needed us, perhaps you do, too.

Please make notes in this book. Dog-ear the pages, or use Post-it® notes all over. When you're done, make a list of all the things you want to discuss further with your tax pro. Get a good tax professional who understands the tax laws related to things you want to accomplish. And most importantly, get a tax pro who will listen to you—as long as you are willing to pay for the time.

Now let's get started on your journey to explore the Internal Revenue Code and its related body of law, in all its glory!

CHAPTER 2

Record-Keeping Tips and Tools That Help Maximize Deductions

A**RE YOU SERIOUS ABOUT** paying less in taxes? I mean, really serious? Believe it or not, you are in control of how much you pay to Uncle Sam, your state, your property tax assessor, city taxes, sales taxes, and all taxes. Look at it this way: you have three choices when it comes to taxes.

You can be a **Tax Pushover**, coasting along and paying out everything that's demanded of you without another thought. You can be a **Tax Vigilante**, fighting passionately to eliminate or reduce taxes wherever you can. Or you can be **Tax Aware**, doing the fundamental, logical things needed to keep your taxes legally low without becoming obsessed. This book will provide you with the information you need to fulfill any of those options. You'll get some routine ideas, but you will find special gems not found anywhere else. They are legal, but most people have never thought about using these strategies and tips.

Tip #1:

The foundation for all tax reporting is good record keeping. The concept is the same whether you're in business or simply dealing with your personal tax situation. In this book, we will focus on your personal records. It's not as hard to do as you think—especially with all the nifty apps available to you. We will talk more about apps in a few minutes.

We won't go into detail on the various apps—that would require a whole other book. The tips that follow provide you with the names and URLs of the top apps that can help make your lives easier. Some are free. Some charge a fee.

Tip #2:

One of the big secrets to getting the best tax benefits is having complete records of all your financial transactions. That way, even if you didn't know about a tax break in your favor, you can take advantage of it at tax time because you have the records to prove you spend the money, drove the miles, or took the appropriate action.

Tip #3:

Everyone should know at least a little bit about the household records. I often find that when it comes to married couples, only one person seems to handle all the household finances. It's important for both to be involved and to know where all the files and records are located. After all, heaven forbid, if you should become divorced or widowed, it's important to know how to take over and manage the household finances, pay bills, get organized for taxes, and so on. These events generally happen suddenly—with no warning at all. I have seen too many people in these situations become paralyzed and unable to manage. As a result, they stop filing tax returns and get into financial and credit trouble for five years or more. Please avoid that, OK? To learn a little bit about bookkeeping, painlessly—and perhaps for free—see the following:

The Bean Counter: http://www.dwmbeancounter.com
The Bookkeeping Master: https://www.youtube.com/
   watch?v=IhYJbCAcCKE

Tip #4:

Income requirements. Here's the information you must store in your records in order to satisfy the dreaded IRS when it comes to income (as it applies to your particular financial situation). We'll discuss many of these in the chapters to come:

- Paystubs—especially the final, year-to-date paystub at the end of the year (just in case you don't end up getting a W-2) or at the end of a job if you leave during the year.
- W-2s, 1099s, 1098s, K-1s, and all other third-party notifications.
- Bank and brokerage statements. Keep a paper or electronic copy of each statement for each and every bank account. That includes PayPal, Itex, Bitcoin, and all other online accounts—including investment accounts.
- Securities trades—sales, purchases, short sales, straddles, and so on. You are the best source of information about the basis of your securities.
- Business income. Do not rely on 1099-MISCs. It's is *your* responsibility to keep your own books when you have a business. Just make sure the total of the 1099s you receive is less than or equal to the business income you report.
- Distributions from partnerships.

- Alimony, unemployment, state refunds, disability, and other miscellaneous sources—often forgotten, but generally taxable.

- Rental income—on your commercial or residential real estate, or your own home, or rooms in your home via private or commercial sources or places like AirBnB.

- Retirement income—Social Security, IRA and retirement account withdrawals.

- Sales of assets. Not all sales are taxable, but all must be reported.

- Awards, prizes, scholarships—surprise, surprise, surprise. Not only are these things often taxable, but when children receive them, they might be subject to kiddie tax (tax at the parents' highest tax bracket).

- Gambling income. Even if you lost the W-2G the casino or gambling establishment gave you, the IRS has a copy of it.

- Barter income—whether through formal clubs or informal barter. Some of the transactions might be taxable. And some of the reported transactions might have deductible offsets.

- Inheritances and gifts. Often there is no taxable income until the assets you receive are sold or cashed out, but there may be some reporting required.

- Hobby income. Sources could be eBay, ePage, Etsy, or other hobby income sites. There are special rules for reporting hobby income and deductions. You're going to hate these particular rules.

- Cancelled debt—on credit cards, real estate, and personal debt. I hate to tell you, but this invisible income is taxable.

- Jury pay. It's not much. And you often return it to your employer, but . . . remember to enter it because the IRS knows.

Tip #5:

Expense requirements. Here's the information you must store in your records in order to satisfy the dreaded IRS when it comes to expenses (as it applies to your particular financial situation):

- Keep copies of all your cancelled checks—even if it's only a PDF copy.

- If you pay cash for something major, get a receipt and scan it into your online filing system or file it into your paper file.

- If you pay cash for something minor like parking, valet, tips, and so on, keep a small pad of paper handy (or 1″ × 1″ Post-it). Write the date, time, location, and amount on a separate page for each instance. File it or scan it by the end of each day.

- When it comes to charity, never pay cash. Always use a check, credit card, or online payment (like PayPal). Get a formal receipt for all donations of $250 or more. (More detail later in Chapter 10: Charity Deductions Begin at Home.)

- Credit card statements are not enough to prove what you bought if you want to deduct it. You need the receipt as well. For big-ticket items, be sure to keep the receipts. (Besides, it helps for returns and warranties.)

- Save your property tax and vehicle registration bills with all the details they show. It doesn't hurt to copy the check or electronic payment and keep it with those receipts.

- Make a copy of every estimated tax payment you make for the IRS, state, or local taxes. Be sure to show the form number, year (or quarter), and type of tax you have just paid.

- Keep mileage logs for all driving so you can later deduct medical, charity, volunteer, moving, and/or business miles.

- When it comes to home improvements, always keep copies of all the invoices and proofs of payment. The details may come in handy for tax credits, warranties, or reducing profits when you sell the property.
- If you get tips on your job, keep the details about the tips you get and those you share with other workers at your job.
- For more details on how to keep records, read chapter 1 of IRS Publication 17—Your Federal Income Tax (https:// www.irs.gov/publications/p17/pt01.html).

How long should you keep records? This is one of the most common questions people ask TaxMama.

Tip #6:

You don't need to keep everything forever . . . but do keep tax returns forever. People are often shocked when the IRS or state pops up saying a tax return has never been filed for a given year, five or ten years ago. Without a copy of that tax return, it's nearly impossible to prove that you did file. They don't take up much space. You can even scan them (preferably as PDF files), as long as you are certain that the copies are clean, readable, and retrievable a decade from now. Do you need all the backup records that went with the tax return? Not necessarily. But keep those for at least six to seven years.

Tip #7:

The IRS is generally only permitted to audit for up to three years after you file a tax return. However, if you have underreported gross income, overreported expenses, or have overstated the basis of assets by 25 percent or more, the IRS has the right to audit for up to six years. If there are criminal omissions or overstatements, the IRS may audit forever. But that should not apply to you. Add one to two years for state deadlines. What about other records?

Tip #8:

Keep the following records until at least six years after the contracts or terms expire or assets are sold:

- Copies of all contracts, warranties, original insurance contracts, and loans. You will need these to ensure that the terms are met in the event you need to file a claim or a dispute. The (annual) invoices aren't enough. The original contracts contain the terms.

- Purchase documents for real estate, and all improvements to the real estate. These will help you when you sell the property—or if you want to convert it to a rental.

- Copies of the original property's purchase and sale, and the tax return reporting of the rollover if you ever rolled over gains—in either tax-free exchanges or the sale of a home—before 1998. (If you don't have the records, start digging.)

- Purchase information and all splits of all stocks or securities that you are still holding (or sold this year). If you reinvested dividends, don't forget to add those reinvestments to the cost. If you don't have all the details, but know approximately when you originally bought the stock, www .netbasis.com can reconstruct the entire history of your ownership and compute your basis for a small fee.

- Deductions for funding a regular Individual Retirement Account (IRA). Sometimes, though, you make after-tax contributions. Be sure to track those, since those funds won't be taxable when you withdraw your money. Also, states may have a different allowable IRA deduction. So you might have a tax basis for the state. (More details in Chapter 11.)

Tip #9:

Keep tax preparation records for at least six years. That means all the cancelled checks, receipts, and records that were directly used in the preparation of your tax return. This should include copies of all your notes, work papers, and correspondence with your tax professional or tax software company. Keep them with a copy of the tax return, so if you're ever audited, everything is right there, right at hand.

> **TAXMAMA'S RECORD-KEEPING LAW OF THE UNIVERSE:**
>
> You won't need to look at most of your records for years. But as soon as you throw something out–you will need it desperately.

Tip #10:

The benefits of mobile applications:

- They let you scan documents, checks, and receipts on the spot and let you upload them to your application instantly instead of spending your entire evening tediously entering data into a traditional print or electronic system. Yawn.

- They generally integrate with other tools to help you organize the data—or to have someone else organize the data for you (like Shoeboxed.com).

- The information can be stored in the Cloud, so you don't need to worry about losing the data, fires, messy desks, and so on.

- When the documents are linked to specific lines in your books and records, you are creating an "audit trail." That means if the IRS or state wants to see the receipt for a particular deduction (or category of deductions), you can just click and give it to them or print out the all the data in the category.

- Some of them will use GPS to track your mileage for each driving incident, allowing you to categorize the trip as personal, business, medical, moving, or charitable mileage. Others will require manual entries for each trip.

Tip #11:

The drawbacks of mobile applications:

- A warning about free apps—read the contract information *carefully*. You will learn that you generally don't own your data. They can shut down the app at any time. Think about this: If they aren't getting paid, how can they afford to keep providing your free service? What are they selling to get the funds to keep their doors open? Are they selling your data to advertisers? Is there a paid upgrade? What about the security of your private information, especially when you link these free apps to your bank accounts and brokerage accounts? Do they have access to your financial usernames and passwords? Who owns and/or creates the apps? Do they have deep pockets to compensate you or help you in the event of identity theft?

- Security—Some of the data are often also stored on your mobile device. You don't generally have it password protected when you use it all day. So the data are at risk. If your device is lost or stolen, you must scramble to change all the passwords on all your accounts *immediately*.

Tip #12:

These are some of the top applications available to you for record keeping and mileage (listed in alphabetical order, not by preference):

DeductR: http://deductr.com
Expensify: https://www.expensify.com
FreshBooks: http://www.freshbooks.com
MetroMile's mileage app: https://www.metromile.com/
technology

Tip #13:

These are some of the top personal record-keeping systems that provide full bookkeeping (listed in alphabetical order, not by preference). Many apps are designed to integrate with these systems:

Mint: https://www.mint.com
Outright: http://outright.com
QuickBooks: http://www.quickbooks.com/App
Quicken: http://www.quicken.com/stay-connected-your
-money
Shoeboxed: https://www.shoeboxed.com

Note: Of course you can use Excel if you know how. But if you don't already know how to use Excel, an app might be a better choice.

Tip #14:

Not everyone lives in the Cloud. Some people still like the feel, texture, and smell of good, old fashioned paper. Here are some paper alternatives for folks who still like the tangible feel of paper records:

Tax MiniMiser is a system with sets of monthly envelopes to hold all your receipts, invoices, and documents—and where you can record all money you receive and money that you spend. Of all the paper systems, the Tax Mini-Miser is the newest one, designed right around the turn of this century (2000) by Bob Whitaker after he got tired of being audited repeatedly. (All the other systems have been used for fifty to one hundred years or more.) http:// taxminimiser.com.

Dome Record Books have books for a variety of industries that include bookkeeping information, bank reconciliations, payroll record, or whatever you need. http://www .domeproductsonline.com/dome-books.

Wilson Jones has been producing columnar pads and binders in many shapes and sizes since 1893. You can design your own journals and ledgers based on the information you need to track. Pair these pads with loose-leaf notebooks and a set of tabs, and voila! You have your own customized accounting system. http://www.wilsonjones .com/wj/us/us/s/2252/accounting-suppliesaspx.

SafeGuard One-Write Systems combines ledger sheets with carbon-backed checks and receipts. So each time you write a check or make a sale, the entry appears on your ledgers without having to copy it over. This is how I first learned bookkeeping and how to reconcile books. https://www.gosafeguard.com/business.

Accordion files can be paired with colorful labels, allowing you to customize your own filing system. Get a file with 24–31 pockets to store your receipts, invoices, and so on. Use a set with 12 pockets to store bank and brokerage statements. Or use the 12 pockets as a tickler file to remind you about monthly bills to pay, things to do, appointments or deadlines, or even birthdays and special occasions.

CHAPTER 3

Should You Prepare Your Own Tax Return?

WHETHER YOU'RE A TAX Pushover, Tax Vigilante, or Tax Aware, the odds are better than 50-50 that you are among the 77 million plus Americans working with a tax professional. But another 70 million or so folks are doing it themselves. In many cases, where your financial life is straightforward and uncomplicated, you're much better off preparing your own tax return. The IRS and all the major tax software companies even make free filing available for you. You will find two different free systems offered through the IRS right here: https://www.irs.gov/uac/Free-File:-Do-Your-Federal-Taxes-for-Free. *Note: The main problem with these free services is that they don't maintain your data files from year to year. So be sure to download and save all your data.*

Tip #15:

File a tax return no matter what. Although the IRS discourages people from filing if they do not have taxable income, have refunds coming to them, or owe any write-in-type taxes, it is in your best interest to file every year. Why? For at least four reasons. Typically, you can file for free, so don't forgo filing.

1. When you file a tax return, the IRS has three years to question your filing. (Add another year or two for your state.) When you file a tax return, they cannot come back to you years later saying you had income that should have been reported. It's hard to prove you didn't need to file when you no longer have records.

2. It's quite possible that you do need to file, to report and pay 2008 Homebuyer's Credit repayments of up to $500 per year, and this will stay in effect until 2024 or until you pay back your entire Homebuyer's Credit. You must also file to report your income information if you received any advance premium credits on your health insurance.

3. If there is a 1099 issued showing any income under your Social Security number that you have not reported, you will be notified by the IRS within weeks after you file. This system helped us find more than $100,000 in bank accounts belonging to a client's Alzheimer's-afflicted sister. Her sister was not in any condition to tell us where her bank accounts were.

4. Via the IRS notification, you will also learn about identity theft—illegals (or even relatives) using your Social Security number to work, or folks filing fraudulent tax returns to generate illegal refunds. The elderly are often targets because people know you won't be filing and won't know you have been targeted for identity theft.

Tip #16:

You are a good candidate for preparing your taxes yourself if you fulfill the following requirements:

- Your only income is from wages, regular pensions, Social Security income, and interest income.
- You have routine dividends—nothing complicated.
- You have IRA contributions with no recharacterizations, and you've been keeping track of any basis (after-tax dollars contributed).
- You have a modest mortgage and uncomplicated property taxes.
- You have children with valid Social Security numbers and with documented child care expenses.
- You have a receipt for every single charitable contribution you make.
- Your children are in college but don't have jobs or scholarships or income of their own that might prompt them to file their own tax returns.

You *must* file a tax return if you received advance credits from the Health Care system. **A tax return may be required** if you received the benefit of advance premium tax credit payments. You must file a tax return to reconcile the amount of advance credit payments made on your behalf with the amount of your actual premium tax credit. You must file an income tax return for this purpose even if you are otherwise not required to file a return (see http://content.govdelivery.com/accounts/USIRS/bulletins/1246e5b).

Tip #17:

The IRS's Free File Alliance system has teamed up with more than a dozen major tax software companies to offer free filing of IRS and some state tax returns. Eligibility is generally based on certain income limits (around $62,000 or so), age, disability, and military service. You can find the list here: http://freefilealliance.org/free-file-alliance-members.

The reason I am telling you about this free service is that about 100 million American taxpayers are eligible, yet only about 43 million tax returns have been filed via the system since 2003. That averages about 3 million tax returns each year. Many people who could use this entirely free service are wasting it. Yes . . . free. No up-sells, no product pitches, nothing.

The only potential charge? If your state doesn't participate in the program, you will have to pay to efile your state return. Get started here: https://apps.irs.gov/app/freeFile.

Tip #18:

Are you very computer savvy? You can get your IRS tax return filed for free without tapping into the commercial databases at all. The IRS has a Free File Fillable Forms system that's a bit clunkier than the commercial software. It's harder to use. But engineers and tech wizards love playing with this system: http://www.irs.gov/uac/Before-Starting-Free-File-Fillable-Forms. You won't get any state filing from this system, but you might want to explore your state's website and see if they have anything similar. Google your state's income tax department for more information or call and ask them if they have online filing software.

Tip #19:

The third free filing option comes from the tax software companies themselves. They all have a certain level of tax return they will file for free. You just start entering your tax return data at the free level. If all your information qualifies for the free service, you're all done. They will efile for free. Some states might be included in the process. Many are not.

If your entries start reaching the point where you need to pay for the tax return, you won't have to start over. You will get a notice that you have entered data on forms or schedules that require having you pay for the return. Then it's up to you to decide if you want to continue.

The good news is, even if you do continue and then decide not to use their services to file the tax return, you won't have to pay them. They only charge you when you get ready to file the return.

On the other hand, sometimes, by paying at the beginning, you can lock in early-bird discounts.

Tip #20:

One of the big advantages to using paid services is that they retain your tax returns in their online database for at least three years. (Some companies archive the data even longer—just ask them if you need it.) You can roll over certain information into the new year—like all the names, addresses, dependents, Social Security numbers, childcare providers, and such. In addition, if you have carryovers from rentals, home offices, and other issues, the new file should have the prior-year amounts. This is one of the best reasons to select a software company and stay with it, year after year.

Tip #21:

H&R Block. Some of TaxMama's Enrolled Agent Exam students work in those offices and I have seen how professional they are. I would trust them with anything. The in-person services can come with high fees. However, their online services offer interesting benefits. For instance, all paid tax returns come with full audit protection, called "Worry-Free Audit Support." If you get audited, they will not only guide you (like the other software companies do); they will provide an Enrolled Agent to represent you at your audit. (Most other companies offer a similar service if you pay an additional $40 or so per tax year.) The other interesting service is their "Best of Both" product. You pretty much have to know about this—it's not all that easy to find on their website. This lets you get all the benefits of entering all your own data, paying a flat fee for the tax return (under $150 for IRS and one state), with an H&R Block tax pro to answer your unlimited questions. They will review your tax return data and make corrections and adjustments, explaining what you did wrong or how to handle complicated issues. They will sign your tax return and efile it for you. For complex returns, this service is much better than anything you can get in their office. They will spend more time with you, if needed, than an office appointment; you will spend substantially less money; and it comes with the audit support.

Tip #22:

TurboTax. TurboTax gives you access to your tax return files for at least four years. Their claim to fame is that they have made it possible to upload data to their system from more than 300,000 financial resources—W-2s, 1099s, bank data, brokerage data, capital gains systems, and more. You can import data from Quicken, QuickBooks, and Mint.com. Better yet, practically everything can be started using your mobile devices. Extensions have traditionally been free. And they claim that two-thirds of filers qualify to prepare their tax returns for free. A few years ago, they started their "Ask the Tax Pro" service as a free service. It has evolved over the years. It's now called their "Expert Service." Now, in order to get access to the Enrolled Agent, or CPA, who answers your questions, you will need to pay for your tax return first. Some of my friends and EA Exam Course graduates have worked for this service—and they are passionate and dedicated to providing useful and accurate information. Last year, because there were so many problems with the new tax issues related to the ObamaCare programs, everyone was very frustrated with the input. In fact, millions of people got bad data on their Form 1095-A and the IRS announced that they would waive penalties for 2014 tax returns on this issue. Unfortunately, customers took out their anger on the TurboTax Answer folks, giving them bad evaluations. Please don't blame those who are helping you navigate the laws because you're angry with the laws. Congress passes them and the IRS only enforces those rules. Let your representatives know. (See my website for information on how to contact all the key players: http://taxmama .com/special-reports/call-to-action.)

Tip #23:

Your least expensive tax software option is TaxAct.com. Their highest priced service costs less than $35, including one state. Most of their support is via email or online chat. But they have excellent resources. One other really great tool they have is for nonfilers. Their website provides access to prior-year software for individuals and businesses as far back as 2008. (Shhh . . . don't tell anyone, but H&R Block tried to buy them up several years ago. In 2011, the US Department of Justice prevented the purchase due to antitrust issues: http://www.justice .gov/file/498231/download.)

Tip #24:

Three other top software options. CompleteTax.com, 1040 .com, and TaxSlayer.com used to have very low prices. Due to all the new complexities and reprogramming needed for Obamacare, as well as protecting against identity theft and fraudulent tax returns, their prices have risen to more than $50 to efile both a federal and state tax return. They are all highly reliable and reputable companies with solid tax research behind them—and members of the IRS Free File Alliance.

Tip #25:

Warning! **While you may find new companies popping up offering great prices for online tax preparation, please be careful.** The information you enter to prepare your tax returns is exactly the kind of information needed for identity theft. So if you have never heard of the company and they don't spell out who is behind these great prices, avoid them. Try to stick with the list of companies on the IRS's Free File Alliance (https://www .freefilealliance.org) list—even if you are using their paid services. You know the IRS has been working with them for years.

CHAPTER 4

Choosing a Tax Professional

A S THE PREVIOUS CHAPTER pointed out, millions upon millions of people can, and do, prepare their own tax returns. But should you? Let's explore criteria for why you may need to consult a tax professional, as well as what kind of tax professional you should hire if you need one.

Tip #26:

Financial issues that require a professional. Don't prepare your own tax returns if you have these issues in your financial life:

- A business of any kind—whether it's as a sole proprietor, partnership, corporation, LLC, farm, ranch, multilevel marketing, network marketing, affiliate sales, pyramid schemes, and so on.

- Hobby income—whether you believe it's a business or not.

- Disability income, workers compensation, or other insurance proceeds that you're not certain are not taxable.

- Lump sum income from Social Security Disability or SSI (after several years) or pensions.

- You are (or a family member is) age 72 or over and have IRAs and/or pension accounts. They require mandatory distributions.

- Divorce, alimony, child support, family support, or disputes about dependents.

- Dependents who don't live at home, who are out of the United States, who don't have Social Security numbers, ITINs, ATINs, or other US-identifying numbers.

- Complicated investments including short sales, wash sales, stock splits, PFICs, flipped real estate, racehorses, and other things you may not understand all that well. If you don't know what the initials stand for or what something means, don't invest in it without consulting a tax pro first.

- Sales of any assets at all—especially real estate, business assets, collectibles, and eBay-type sales.

- Rental real estate of any kind, like roommates, bed and breakfast, short-term rentals (like AirBnB), studio rentals, time-share rentals, and so on.

- You are a first-time home-buyer.

- Complicated mortgage issues—you refinanced with balances higher than the original loan, loan modifications, balances over $1 million, multiple homes, private lenders, or your name is not on the loan or title.

- Scholarships, stipends, grants, prizes, winnings of any kind.

- Kiddie tax issues that you may not even realize you have.

- Gambling winnings and losses—casinos, clubs, bingo, lottery, and so on.

- Employee business expenses.

- Investment interest and other investment expenses.

- Complicated or high charitable contributions—especially for volunteer work, donations of high-value goods (art, vehicles, securities, more than $1,000 of clothing and household goods), and other things that require more substantiation, appraisals, or expertise.

- Military service—there are special benefits for both state and federal you don't want to miss.

- Disasters, casualties, forced easements—whether personal or business, all have special benefits you can use to your advantage.

- Gifts that you made or received of $14,000 or more per person to/from any individual, including money you received from crowdfunding sources like GoFundMe, KickStarter, and so on.

- You have ownership or signature authority over any financial accounts overseas—whether for yourself, your (elderly) parents or clan, your children, an estate, trust, or business. You own a share of the family business. You have a vacation home outside the United States.

- You have any extra taxes, like the Net Investment Income Tax (NIIT), the extra Medicare tax on wages or self-employment income, household employee taxes, excise taxes, and so on.

- You might be entitled to tax credits for your child(ren), low income, education, energy, retirement, or a whole raft of other things you might not know are available to you from the IRS and/or your state.

- If you have any questions and really want to sit down and talk to a tax professional.

Tip #27:

All paid preparers must have a Professional Tax Identification Number (PTIN). There are more than 700,000 US tax professionals with PTINs. In 2015, the IRS launched their database of all PTIN'd tax professionals. You can look up your tax pro here: http://irs.treasury.gov/rpo/rpo.jsf. If the tax pro you are paying is not in the database, you can contact the IRS Office of Professional Responsibility (OPR) by sending an email to epp@irs.gov and providing the name, address, business name, and any other specific information you have about this individual. The IRS will let you know if there is an error in the database or if this person is operating illegally. You can also contact the IRS OPR to get more information about a tax pro's status if they are not in the database.

Tip #28:

Signature requirements. Sometimes tax professionals use TurboTax or some other consumer software to prepare your tax returns and don't sign your tax return as the preparer. That tax professional is operating illegally. You can report that person to the IRS by filing a Form 14157. You can find more information on the IRS website here: https://www.irs.gov/Tax-Professionals/Make-a-Complaint-About-a-Tax-Return-Preparer. Incidentally, if you think this person has been squirreling away a lot of money or preparing fraudulent returns, consider turning them in to the IRS for a reward. Use Form 211: https://www.irs.gov/pub/irs-pdf/f211.pdf.

Tip #29:

Volunteer tax preparation services. This is the one category of tax professionals who will not be in the database, who do not need valid PTINs, and who will not sign your tax returns. If you meet certain income and/or age criteria you can get **free** in-person tax preparation and tax problem resolution from these sources. You may have heard about these programs. To find a VITA or TCE site in your area, please call 800-906-9887.

- VITA—Volunteer Income Tax Assistance centers help people who earn less than $53,000 (indexed for inflation), are elderly, have disabilities, have trouble with English, or are military families. Volunteers can prepare and efile returns and help with fundamental returns, including a variety of credits like the Earned Income Credit, Child Tax Credits, and Retirement Credit.

- TCE—Tax Counseling for the Elderly centers will help se-niors with all the same things as VITA does. In addition, TCE provides counseling on a number of issues related to retirement, Social Security, and other government-related issues—and can help seniors avoid scams. TCE centers are often run by AARP (American Association of Retired Persons) at their Tax-Aide locations. You can find them all over the country: http://www.aarp.org/money/taxes/aarp _taxaide/. For more information, call 888-687-2277.

- AFTC—The Armed Forces Tax Council provides tax as-sistance specifically for members of the military and their families. They have on-base coordinators, worldwide, for the Marine Corps, Air Force, Army, Navy, and Coast Guard. Both the IRS and the states offer quite a number of special deferrals, allowances, and benefits for active-duty service people and their families. So, if possible, use the AFTC advisors to help you. To get more information, ask your commanding officer or call the main IRS phone num-ber at 1-800-829-1040.

- LITC—Most people have never heard of these Low In-come Taxpayer Clinics. They are overseen by the National

Taxpayer Advocate Service. Often affiliated with colleges or universities, LITCs offer free or low-cost services to taxpayers in trouble. They represent low-income individuals in disputes with the Internal Revenue Service, including audits, appeals, collection matters, and federal tax litigation. LITCs can also help taxpayers respond to IRS notices and correct account problems. Some LITCs provide education about taxpayer rights and responsibilities for low-income taxpayers and taxpayers who speak English as a second language (ESL). Use the LITC map to find one in your area: http://www.taxpayeradvocate.irs.gov/about/litc.

Tip #30:

How many kinds of tax professionals are there? These are the main categories of tax preparation and consultation professionals you should choose from. (Numbers in parentheses are the PTIN holders in each category):

- Enrolled agents (EA; more than 50,000)—EAs are the nation's tax specialists, with the highest credential that the IRS issues to tax professionals. They are licensed to work anywhere in the country and overseas, with respect to your IRS and state issues. They must complete an average of 24 hours of tax education every year (30 hours if they are a member of the National Association of Enrolled Agents). They are a perfect choice if you need individual and business tax preparation, tax planning, tax audit representation, or you have tax debts. These are their areas of specialty. Some EAs also handle estates, trusts, and nonprofit organizations. Many also offer bookkeeping and payroll services year-round.

- Certified public accountants (CPA; more than 213,000)— CPAs are the best-known tax professionals. They are licensed by their state CPA society and/or consumer affairs departments. Their practice tends to be limited to their own state unless another state offers reciprocity. However, the IRS will accept their credentials anywhere in the United States or overseas. CPAs must also get continuing professional education, but there is no mandatory tax education requirement. Most CPAs prepare all kinds of tax returns. Some are adept at IRS audits, while a few are skilled at tax debt representation. So if you have that kind of problem, ask about their experience first. CPAs are great if you have a high-value business—especially if you are hoping to go public one day. For many CPA firms, write-up (accounting) is their lifeblood. Some firms primarily prepare tax returns for their business clients, related parties, and referrals. They are excellent if you have a nonprofit organization, which often requires an annual audit. Some offer certified audit services.

- Tax attorneys (more than 31,000)—These people are also licensed by their state Bar and/or state consumer affairs agencies. Like CPAs, their practice tends to be limited to their own state, unless another state offers reciprocity. However, the IRS will accept their credentials anywhere in the US or overseas. Like CPAs, attorneys must also get continuing professional education, but there is no mandatory tax education requirement. You generally do not need an attorney to prepare your personal tax return. Some tax attorneys (often members of the American Bar Association Tax Section [http://www.americanbar.org/groups/taxation .html]) will have extensive, complex, high-level tax backgrounds and continuing education. Use attorneys for estate and gift planning, business succession planning, and criminal tax issues. You need their help on all contracts and agreements, especially with respect to real estate, business agreements, trusts, wills, and so on. You don't generally need a tax attorney to help you with IRS debts. EAs and CPAs can help you with that. You might need an attorney to represent you on complex foreign bank account and asset issues. However, some EAs and CPAs can help with the noncriminal areas of foreign account reporting.

- State-licensed professionals—Of all fifty of the United States, only three have any licensing requirements for tax professionals. They are California, Oregon, and Maryland. Tax preparers in these states must pass a test and take a certain number of hours of continuing education in taxes and ethics each year. If you live in one of these states, make sure your tax preparer is either licensed by the state or is an EA, CPA, or attorney. *Note: Attorneys and CPAs licensed in other states, but practicing in CA, OR, or MD, may have to register with these states' tax preparer programs.* No one else may charge you to prepare a tax return. These tax professionals are limited to preparing a tax return and to answering the IRS's or state's questions about the tax return that they prepared. That's it. They are not permitted to represent you at any levels of the IRS with respect to balances due, collections, appeals, notices, or anything else. However, they may be able to help with some of your state tax department issues.

- Annual Filing Season Program Certificate of Completion (AFSP; more than 43,000)—In 2014, the IRS instituted a voluntary program to allow unlicensed tax professionals in 47 states to demonstrate a higher level of training and expertise. These people have all the same rights as the state-licensed preparers when it comes to dealing with the IRS. They may represent you at IRS audits on the tax returns they prepared. They cannot speak for you before the IRS collections or appeals divisions.

- Unlicensed tax professionals who have PTINs (more than 375,000)—These people are permitted to prepare your tax return and to file your tax return electronically. Period. Some are highly experienced and do get a great deal of education and training throughout the year. Many are not, so beware. To determine if the unlicensed tax professional of your choice is reliable, here are some steps to take:

- Check that IRS PTIN database I mentioned previously. If it shows that their PTIN is in good standing, that's good news.

- Ask if they are a member of any professional tax organizations. Some reputable organizations include the National Association of Enrolled Agents (NAEA), National Association of Tax Professionals (NATP), National Society of Accountants (NSA), National Association of Tax Consultants (NATC), and American Society of Tax Problem Solvers (ASTPS), among others: https://www.taxsites .com/associations.html. All these organizations require their members to maintain high standards of continuing education.

Tip #31:

Avoid tax preparation outfits within certain retail establishments. Services offered at car lots, stereo stores, and other high-ticket stores where they provide free or low-cost tax preparation services are often really designed to help you get a refund to use toward a store purchase. The preparers may be unlicensed, untrained, and only know how to generate high refunds in ways that may not be legal.

Tip #32:

Avoid tax offices that push refund anticipation loans (RAL)—especially if they tell you that you must get one. With current IRS efiling protocols, you will probably get your refund deposited directly to your bank account within about ten business days or less. So there is absolutely no need to pay someone a high fee to get your own money. The IRS frowns on this practice and has posted alerts to the public about what to watch out when being offered RALs: http://www.irs.gov/uac/Tax-Refund-Related-Products.

Tip #33:

Read your tax return before you sign it. By law, all tax preparers must give you a copy of your tax return before you sign the Form 8879 or Form 8453 to file electronically. It doesn't have to be on paper; an electronic copy is OK. But do take the time to read and review it before you sign the electronic filing forms or before mailing in your paper tax return. If the preparer made an error, it's your problem and your responsibility. So read the whole return and ask questions if you don't understand something.

Tip #34:

Amazing and magical refunds are too good to be true. Some unscrupulous preparers attract clients by promising huge refunds. They make up numbers on Schedule A, Itemized Deductions—like mortgage interest (even when you don't own a home), tax credits like the American Opportunity Credit for education costs, or other credits that don't apply to you. If your refund is strangely high, ask them how it got that way. Do not file a fraudulent tax return. If you do, the IRS will catch you. You will face all the original taxes, plus high penalties and interest on the taxes and penalties. The preparer? He or she will be long gone and impossible to find.

Tip #35:

Find a tax pro with whom you can establish a long-term relationship. Get to know this person and return to that firm year after year. In fact, since it's difficult to do tax planning during the tax preparation appointment, schedule a planning appointment for May or June so you can discuss your financial goals, planned large purchases, or expenses (home, dental work, college, retirement, etc.).

Tip #36:

Always call your tax pro for a consultation before you take any large step financially. It breaks our hearts when you call after you have already done something. We can help guide you before the fact and often help you find a tax-free way to use your retirement funds or make investments or get credits. Once you've already taken the step, fixing it may be impossible—or time-consuming and expensive. Believe me, that one-hour consultation in advance may save you thousands of dollars later.

CHAPTER 5

Deductions around the House

THE AMERICAN DREAM—OWN YOUR own home, a car or two, a big screen television, and several mobile communications devices. It's true, not everyone ends up buying a home, but those who do are entitled to a whole raft of itemized deductions and, perhaps, even tax credits. First, let's take them in the order they appear on Schedule A. Then we'll explore the potential credits and how to snag them.

Tip #37:

Real property taxes. Deduct the real estate taxes you pay on all your properties, unless some of those taxes are deducted elsewhere. This split deduction might happen if you use a home partially for business (Form 8829) or rent out a room or half a duplex (Schedule E). Read your property tax bill carefully because not all the charges are deductible as property taxes. For instance, your bill might include special assessments for bonds, or might include sewer fees or payments for city or county improvements. While you pay for those things along with your property taxes, they are technically not deductions. (Shhh . . . I have never seen the IRS adjust for this on audit.) Some states might have special charges that look like nondeductible assessments or fees but are deductible. For instance, California has something called Mello-Roos fees. In February 2012, the IRS ruled that these are deductible as property taxes. *Note: If you pay your taxes to your lender as part of your monthly payment, they will give you a year-end statement showing the taxes, property insurance, and PMI (mortgage insurance) paid on your behalf during the year.*

Tip #38:

In order to deduct the property taxes, you must own the property and you must be the person making the payments. Gosh, that seems obvious, doesn't it? Why bring it up? Because sometimes people don't have enough of their own credit to buy their homes. Someone else needs to get the loan for them (like a parent, relative, or an amazingly good friend). So their name isn't on title—or on the loan. Uh oh. That means the person on title doesn't get the property tax deduction because they weren't the ones paying the property tax. And you don't get the deduction because you're not on title. Is there a solution to this dilemma? Yes there is. Stay tuned to Tip #50, when we talk about mortgages.

Tip #39:

What are the most overlooked, but deductible, property taxes? Property taxes assessed as part of your time-share fees and as part of your community's common area fees. Some sets of fees are pretty low. In other areas, common area fees are quite high, and you can pick up several hundred dollars (or thousands) by getting the reports from your management companies.

Tip #40:

Escrow is another source of real estate taxes paid. When buying or selling real estate, read the HUD-1 summary (or escrow closing statement). You may find that you have paid taxes through the escrow by repaying the sellers for taxes they paid for part of the year. On the other hand, you might learn that they are paying you in advance for their share of the taxes due later in year. For example, many states collect taxes around April and December. The April payment covers the period from January through June. The December payment covers taxes due from July through December. So if the sale takes place in September, the buyer ends up paying the June–September property taxes as part of the December bill. In escrow, the seller makes up for that by paying the buyer for those June–September property taxes. That means the buyer reduces his or her property tax expense at the end of the year. The opposite happens if the property is sold in the first half of the year. The buyer reimburses the seller for the taxes he or she paid in the beginning of the year and gets an extra property tax deduction as a result. Here's where you find this information on the HUD 1 statement: http://portal.hud.gov/hudportal/documents/huddoc?id=1.pdf (see image on page 42).

Tip #41:

Personal property taxes. Typically, these are the annual fees you pay to your state's department of motor vehicles based on the value of your auto, boat, ATV, Jet Ski–type things, motorcycles, snowmobiles, and other such toys and vehicles. If the fee is not based on value but is simply a processing-type fee—the

100. Gross Amount Due from Borrower		400. Gross Amount Due to Seller	
101. Contract sales price		401. Contract sales price	
102. Personal property		402. Personal property	
103. Settlement charges to borrower (line 1400)		403.	
104.		404.	
105.		405.	
Adjustment for items paid by seller in advance		Adjustment for items paid by seller in advance	
106. City/town taxes to		406. City/town taxes to	
107. County taxes to		407. County taxes to	
108. Assessments to		408. Assessments to	
109.		409.	
110.		410.	
111.		411.	
112.		412.	
120. Gross Amount Due from Borrower		420. Gross Amount Due to Seller	
200. Amount Paid by or in Behalf of Borrower		500. Reductions In Amount Due to seller	
201. Deposit or earnest money		501. Excess deposit (see instructions)	
202. Principal amount of new loan(s)		502. Settlement charges to seller (line 1400)	
203. Existing loan(s) taken subject to		503. Existing loan(s) taken subject to	
204.		504. Payoff of first mortgage loan	
205.		505. Payoff of second mortgage loan	
206.		506.	
207.		507.	
208.		508.	
209.		509.	
Adjustments for items unpaid by seller		Adjustments for items unpaid by seller	
210. City/town taxes to		510. City/town taxes to	
211. County taxes to		511. County taxes to	
212. Assessments to		512. Assessments to	

cost is not deductible. Often your license fee includes such base fees or special fees for vanity plates. Those costs are not deductible either. Incidentally, in the many decades that I have been preparing tax returns, this is one of the most often overlooked deductions. For some folks, it may not be much. But for others, when you look at all the vehicles . . . it adds up. Especially since motor home and RV licenses can be deducted on this line (line 7 Schedule A). *Note: If you use the car for business, only report the personal use percentage of these taxes. For instance, if you use the car 80 percent for business, and the tax is $75, only report $15 on Schedule A.*

Tip #42:

Sales taxes. Although these aren't around-the-house-type taxes, let's talk about them anyway—especially since we buy things for the home and pay sales taxes. There's a strategy to use with these deductions. If at all possible, deduct your sales taxes instead of your state income taxes. Why? There are several reasons:

- When you deduct your sales taxes, you don't have to report your state income tax refund as income on the following year's tax return.

- You don't have to track all the sales taxes you paid. Just use the IRS's Sales Tax Calculator: https://www.irs.gov/Individuals/Sales-Tax-Deduction-Calculator.

- Your tax software might even have the information for your state—just add in the extra sales tax percentage your county or parish charges.

- In addition to the sales tax tables, where the tax is based on your AGI, you can add the sales taxes paid on big-ticket items like cars, boats, RV, expensive electronics, Rolex watches, and so on.

- Some states don't even have income taxes, so sales taxes are your only option.

Note: The sales tax deduction is one of those tax provisions that have been expiring every year. This is now a permanent part of the Internal Revenue Code as Section 106 of the PATH Act of 2015. Please see Bonus Tip #270 for more details.

Tip #43:

State income taxes. Naturally, if your state income taxes are much higher than the sales taxes you paid, use this deduction. When you end up getting a refund on your state tax return, after itemizing the taxes on Schedule A, you will need to report all or part of your state refund as income. Why only part of it? Well, if you didn't get any benefit from the state income tax deduction, you don't need to pay taxes on refund, either. There are detailed instructions for line 10 of Form 1040 (https://www.irs.gov/instructions/i1040gi/ar01.html#d0e3584). Generally your software will do this computation for you if you give it enough information about last year's tax return.

Tip #44:

Good news: if you did not itemize in the year for which you received your refund, the state refund is not taxable. For instance, let's say you filed several years' tax returns in 2015—you filed 2012, 2013, and 2014. Suppose you didn't itemize in 2012 and 2013, but your state refund is $10,000. None of that refund is taxable. But let's pretend that you itemized in 2014 and got the full benefit of your state income tax deduction. In that case, the $5,000 refund you received for 2014 is income to you in 2015 even though you may have a received a total of $15,000 in state refunds during 2015.

Tip #45:

Here are three commonly overlooked state tax deduction opportunities:

- If you were making state-estimated tax payments, remember the January payment for the fourth quarter. Even though the payment you made in the tax year you are filing was for last year, you get to deduct it. Why? You paid it in the current tax year.

- Did you have a state overpayment on your tax return that you applied toward the following year's taxes? That's considered a payment you made in the current year. For instance, you applied your 2014 state tax refund to your 2015 state taxes. That payment is considered made in 2015.

- Did you pay a balance due to the state when you filed your tax return? Remember to add that to your total state taxes paid. For instance, you paid your state $532 when you filed your 2014 income tax return in April of 2015. That payment is made in 2015. Oh, and do remember to add it to your total estimated payments for 2015. A lot of people forget to include that.

Tip #46:

Here are two more "state" tax deductions that most people don't know about at all:

- Taxes imposed by Indian tribal governments are deductible. Though I would bet that people living on reservations know this one applies to them, an excerpt from IRS Publication 17 reads:

  "Indian tribal government. An Indian tribal govern-ment recognized by the Secretary of the Treasury as per-forming substantial government functions will be treated as a state for purposes of claiming a deduction for taxes. Income taxes, real estate taxes, and personal property taxes imposed by that Indian tribal government (or by any of its subdivisions that are treated as political subdivisions of a state) are deductible" (https://www.irs.gov/publications/p17/ch22.html#en_US_2014_publink1000173139).

- Foreign income taxes paid are deductible. You may have paid them as deductions from dividends, from your pension, or from the foreign equivalent of Social Security income. Be sure to convert the foreign currency to US dollars. You can look up the IRS's approved currency conversion rates on their website here: https://www.irs.gov/Individuals/International-Taxpayers/Yearly-Average-Currency-Exchange-Rates. Or you can use the Oanda site to get values on specific days or averages for a year or so: http://www.oanda.com/currency/.

○ Incidentally, you have a choice about those foreign taxes. You may take them as a deduction here on Schedule A or you may choose to take them as a tax credit using Form 1116, Foreign Tax Credit.

○ What if you are not reporting your foreign income at all because you are working overseas? If you have the privilege of using Form 2555, the Foreign Earned Income Exclusion, then you may not use any foreign taxes you pay as either a deduction or a credit. After all, if you don't pay taxes in the United States, you don't get any US tax benefits.

Enough about taxes! Let's move on to more interesting things. Like . . . interest!

Tip #47:

Mortgage interest paid. This looks pretty simple, doesn't it? Yet I managed to teach an entire two-hour course on the subject (http://www.cpelink.com/self-study/home-mortgage-interest -deductions/6097). The IRS publishes a 17-page booklet on the subject—IRS Publication 936 (https://www.irs.gov/pub/irs-pdf/ p936.pdf). Let me just give you the high points here. First, the good news: the bad news I am about to give you probably won't impact you. OK, here's the bad news: your mortgage interest deduction is limited in several ways.

• You may only deduct the interest on acquisition debt—the amount of the mortgage you took out when you bought the house. Plus any mortgage you took out to pay for repairs or remodeling.

• In addition, you may deduct the mortgage up to another $100,000 of a home equity line of credit (HELOC). This money may be used for anything—like debt consolidation or the vacation of a lifetime. It doesn't matter what. The loan must be secured by the home.

- Often, when the value of the home increases dramatically or interest rates plunge, people refinance. When you refinance, your mortgage interest deduction is limited to the interest on the balance of the loan at the time of the refinancing plus that HELOC value of $100,000. For instance, your original loan was for $200,000 five years ago, and today the loan balance is $175,000. The house is now worth $400,000. You get a new 80 percent loan for $320,000 and include the points and refinance fees in the new loan, taking the balance to $325,000. Since the interest rates are lower, your payments don't go up very much—but you're able to pull out $145,000 in cash. Suppose this is the only loan on the house. You may deduct the interest on this part of the mortgage only:

> The $175,000 balance left on the original loan
> The $100,000 allowable HELOC
> Total: $275,000 Allowable Mortgage Balance

What happens to the interest on the other $50,000 ($325,000 loan, less the deductible mortgage value of $275,000)? Nothing. No deduction. No carryforward. Nothing. So please take this into account when refinancing. If you are ever audited, the IRS will catch this error and may go back for up to three years to recover taxes due.

- $1 million is the limit of the total amount of mortgage balance on which you may deduct interest. That, plus the $100,000 HELOC. So . . . in total, you may deduct mortgage interest expense on up to $1,100,000. This limit is not per house; it is for all the homes you might own. The IRS had a field day with this limit several years ago. They tested how well taxpayers were adhering to this rule by auditing taxpayers who owned property in Santa Barbara, California, particularly in the Montecito area. Estates in that area sell for millions of dollars. Most of the taxpayers who were audited ended up having taken the full mortgage deduction instead of limiting the interest expense to $1,100,000. Their tax professionals were furious at the IRS (uh, actually at themselves for getting caught in this major blunder). But . . . the law is the law.

• Yet another limit—unlike real property taxes, where you may deduct the property taxes on all your properties, you are only entitled to deduct the interest on up to two homes. So people who have multiple homes must pick the two homes producing the highest interest deduction for the year. Don't worry, you may switch your choices each year. TaxMama suggests that you use the homes with the highest interest rate or highest total interest expense.

• One more limit—Alternative Minimum Tax (AMT) rears its ugly head. Take a look at the AMT form, Form 6251 (https://www.irs.gov/pub/irs-pdf/f6251.pdf). When you deduct any HELOC interest at all, you need to enter that amount on line 4.

This is not an adjustment that your tax software will pick up automatically—most professional software doesn't even pick it up. This entry must be made manually. (Though, if the software companies would just create an input field for HELOC interest, the software would be able to do this for you.)

Part I Alternative Minimum Taxable Income (See instructions for how to complete each line.)

1 If filing Schedule A (Form 1040), enter the amount from Form 1040, line 41, and go to line 2. Otherwise, enter the amount from Form 1040, line 38, and go to line 7. (If less than zero, enter as a negative amount.)   **1**

2 Medical and dental. If you or your spouse was 65 or older, enter the **smaller** of Schedule A (Form 1040), line 4, or 2.5% (.025) of Form 1040, line 38. If zero or less, enter -0-   **2**

- Can you get around these deduction limits by moving some of the interest to your office in home (Form 8829) or to the rental form (Schedule E) when you rent out space in your home? Nope. I thought it would be a terrific loophole and researched this. Sad to say, no matter where you try to move that interest on your personal residence(s), you are still limited to the acquisition debt + $100,000 or to the $1,100,000 total loan balance.

- To top it all off, if you managed to snag a loan with a really good interest rate, like 4 percent or less—a married couple probably won't have enough interest expense to allow you to itemize in the first place. (Average US mortgage debt is around $156,000 [https://www.nerdwallet.com/blog/credit-card-data/average-credit-card-debt-household/] × 4 percent = $6,240. Add in about $2,000 in property taxes and your potential itemized deduction is under $10,000, including state taxes. The standard deduction for a couple filing jointly is more than $12,000.)

Tip #48:

Finally, some good news—here's how you *can* increase the deduction for mortgage interest after you refinance. Suppose you realized that you had $200,000 in equity that you could pull out of your mortgage. This is a great way to get your hands on some cash without having to pay tax on the earnings. You decided that you can use that money as a down payment on a rental property. There is a special provision (https://www.irs.gov/publications/p936/ar02.html#en_US_2014_publink1000229898) that lets you choose to treat that loan not as being secured by your home, but as a loan on the new rental property (deduct the loan on Schedule E). Or you can use that money to invest in your business (deduct the loan on Schedule C or on your business tax return). In any case, the money from the loan must go directly to the business account or property purchase escrow or seller. Try to make sure these funds never hit your personal bank account at all. If the funds must get deposited into your bank account first, consider opening a separate account that you only use for that property or business and deposit this money there. Under no circumstances should these funds get mixed in with your personal funds. Otherwise the IRS does something called "tracing." They trace each check or debit that cleared after the deposit and treat that deposit as being spent on those things (like the dry cleaner, groceries, credit cards, etc.) instead of on your investment. You might want to consider sitting down with a tax professional who is experienced with this area of taxation to work out the details. And consider writing loan documents between yourself and your business or yourself and the rental property to make sure the transaction is kosher. A good real estate attorney can be worth the investment of a consulting fee to ensure you are able to claim these interest deductions in full.

Tip #49:

Often overlooked mortgage interest is the interest on your timeshares. Since most people do not own two homes, they are not subject to all that nonsense we talked about before. But while you may not own an actual vacation home, you probably own a timeshare. Those loans tend to run about ten or twenty years. That is considered a second home. You're entitled to deduct the interest on it.

Very Special Tip #50:

Uh oh . . . the mortgage is not in your name. We started talking about this in Tip #38. You didn't have enough credit to get the loan, so your parents are named on the loan and on the title. Technically you are not allowed to deduct the mortgage interest or property taxes since you don't own the house on paper. You probably get a notice from the IRS each year saying that they don't have a Form 1098 reporting any mortgage interest in your name, and you have to duke it out with them in the mail, year after year. But this is such a common phenomenon these days that there is a solution. (Tax professionals struggle with this problem. Many don't know this definitive solution. They know there should be one, but don't know what the solution is. Now you will know!)

- You are what is called an "Equitable Owner," or "Beneficial Owner." When you respond to the IRS, tell them that you are the Beneficial Owner under Treasury Regulation Treas. Reg. § 1.163-1(b) (https://www.law.cornell.edu/cfr/text/26/1.163-1) and the owner on the title will not be taking the deduction. (Feel free to read the regulation.)

- It might not be a bad idea to also get some paperwork drawn up. Have an attorney draw up a contract between you and the owner on the title, spelling out that you are the actual owner and that they just helped you out for credit purposes.

- Have a deed prepared showing the title in your name. Better yet, have your name added to the title with the named owner. (It's not wise for the person who is responsible for the loan to be removed from title. After all, if you default on the payments, it's their credit on the line. Without being on title, they won't be able to get control of the house and they won't be notified if you default on the loan.)

- If you ever face a tax battle, there's a really good article about this topic in the *Journal of Accountancy* based on Tax Court cases that were won (http://www.journalofaccountancy.com/issues/2008/oct/equitableownerequalsdeduction.htm).

Interest	10	Home mortgage interest and points reported to you on Form 1098	10	
You Paid	11	Home mortgage interest not reported to you on Form 1098. If paid to the person from whom you bought the home, see instructions and show that person's name, identifying no., and address ▶		
Note. Your mortgage interest deduction may be limited (see instructions).		--		
		--	11	
	12	Points not reported to you on Form 1098. See instructions for special rules	12	

Tip #51:

Mortgage interest paid to private lenders. Generally, when you pay a bank or financial institution, they send you a Form 1098 at the end of the year showing how much you paid in interest. It might also include your property taxes, PMI, and insurance payment information. The IRS gets a copy of that and matches it to your tax return. But when you pay a private lender, they don't generally send you a Form 1098. And most individuals do not think of sending the private lender a Form 1099-INT to tell the IRS how much interest you are paying to that person. Instead, there is line 11 on the Schedule A. That's where you give the name, address, and Social Security number (SSN) or other Taxpayer Identification Number (TIN) to the IRS. If you don't have that information, send the lender a Form W-9 to request it (https://www.irs.gov/pub/irs-pdf/fw9.pdf). If you think they will resist providing you with that information, send it certified, with return receipt requested so you can prove that you tried to get it. Then enter all the information you do have with "REFUSED" as the SSN or TIN. *Note: You don't mail the completed W-9 to the IRS. You just keep it in your records for as long as you pay that lender + four years.*

Tip #52:

Unpaid interest. Some loans start out with the buyer's monthly payments being less than the amount of monthly principal and interest. Those are called negatively amortizing loans. While you get a lower payment in the beginning, the unpaid interest gets added to loan balance. Your year-end mortgage statement will show the total amount of interest generated on the loan and the amount that you actually paid. You may only deduct the interest you pay. The unpaid portion will only be deductible when you actually pay it, perhaps several years later.

Tip #53:

Reverse mortgages. A reverse mortgage is a loan where the lender pays you (in a lump sum, a monthly advance, a line of credit, or a combination of all three) while you continue to live in your home. You don't have any mortgage payments. What a relief. With a reverse mortgage, you retain title to your home. Depending on the plan, your reverse mortgage becomes due, with interest, when you move, sell your home, reach the end of a preselected loan period, or die. Because reverse mortgages are considered loan advances and not income, the amount you receive is not taxable. Any interest (including original issue discount) accrued on a reverse mortgage is not deductible until you actually pay it, which is usually when you pay off the loan in full.

Tip #54:

Reverse mortgage warning. While you might be relieved not to have to pay a monthly mortgage payment anymore, beware, and read everything carefully. Anything you don't understand, have them explain, slowly, until you do understand. The interest on the reverse mortgage is generally higher than interest you would normally pay on a regular mortgage. There are a lot of fees they charge that get added to your loan balance. You cannot get any additional cash out of the home if you need it in an emergency. Your reverse mortgage lender controls your equity. If you are married, or have someone you care about (like your child or a friend) living in the home, make sure they are on title before getting the reverse mortgage. Otherwise, if you are forced to move out into a convalescent facility or senior home, they may be kicked out of the house. The lender will demand payment or force the sale of the home when the "owner of record" no longer lives there. So if they are on the title before the loan is issued, they will be protected. But . . . watch out for potential gift and estate tax issues if you add them to title. It would be a good idea to discuss the details about, and alternatives to, reverse mortgages with a tax professional and/or tax attorney.

Tip #55:

Personal residence points. These are the extra fees you typically pay when you get a mortgage. When you buy the home, they are fully deductible. Incidentally, if the points are added to your mortgage and you do not actually pay them, there is no deduction. What if the seller pays your points to help you buy the house? Do you get a deduction? No again. If you don't spend, you don't deduct. If you did pay the points, how can you prove that *you* paid them? Deposit a check for the amount of the points into escrow, or pay it directly to the lender or loan broker. Otherwise . . . there is no deduction at all. Incidentally, if the points are not reported to you on the Form 1098 from your lender, read the instructions to Schedule A and enter those points on line 12 instead of including them on line 10.

Tip #56:

Refinanced points. When you refinance that first mortgage, you must deduct the cost over the life of the mortgage. That is called amortization. If the mortgage is for 30 years, the points are deducted over 360 months. Let's say you refinanced in the beginning of September. That first year, you will deduct 4/360th of the points (September to December = 4 months). From then on, you will deduct 12/360th until the last year when you deduct whatever is left over.

Tip #57:

Refinanced again points. You have already refinanced once, right? You paid $3,000 and have been able to deduct about $250 so far. But you found a better interest rate (or your credit improved) and you can refinance again. OK, you will amortize the new points as we have described. But what do you do about the old points? You still have $2,750 that hasn't been deducted, right? Great news! You may deduct that entire balance, since that loan has been paid off.

Tip #58:

Someone else's points. Sometimes we use incentives to sell our properties. For instance, to close a sale, you offer to pay the buyer's closing costs, including their points. Is that a deduction to you, as the seller? Nope. That is part of the selling price. You add this to your selling costs and it reduces your overall profit on the sale. So you think this comes out the same in the end? Think again. If the profit on your home is under $250,000 (or $500,000 when you file jointly), you won't be paying taxes anyway. So this doesn't matter. And you didn't get the deduction for the points, since it wasn't your loan obligation. But at least you finally got to sell the home and stop paying for that mortgage.

Tip #59:

Private mortgage insurance (PMI; https://www.irs.gov/publications/p936/ar02.html#en_US_2014_publink1000296058). This is insurance that you must pay for if your down payment is too low. It's designed to protect the lenders in case you default. This expense became an allowable deduction sometime around 2007 (https://www.law.cornell.edu/uscode/text/26/163#.Vh_JqivSmSY). However, this is one of those political footballs (like the huge $250 deduction for educators' costs). Each year, Congress needs to reconsider this deduction and extend it—or not. At the time of this writing, the PMI deduction was good for last year but is not yet approved for this year (2015). Oh Good! Congress extended this through December 31, 2016, as part of the Internal Revenue Code as Section 152 of the PATH Act of 2015. Please see Bonus Tip #270 for more details.

What's the fuss all about? After all, when your AGI is higher than $100,000 ($50,000 if married filing separately), your deduction phases out. So why can't Congress make this permanent? Write to your legislators and ask them (http://taxmama.com/special-reports/call-to-action). Meanwhile, before claiming this deduction, please Google the deductibility of PMI each year. That said, just how much *is* deductible?

- You may deduct the premiums you paid in the current year for the current year. In other words, if you paid a large lump sum in advance that covers several years, you may only deduct the premium for the current year.

- You may only deduct PMI on acquisition debt—that is, loans used to buy, build, or improve a home. You may not deduct it when you refinance.

- For veterans who get loans from the Department of Veterans Affairs, it is commonly known as a funding fee. If it is provided by the Rural Housing Service, it is commonly known as a guarantee fee. Regardless of what it's called, it follows all the same rules as private mortgage insurance.

Tip #60:

Make your PMI payment go away! As soon as you can, make this financial drain disappear. When your mortgage balance is 80 percent or less than the value of your home, you can make a written request to your lender to cancel the PMI premiums. How can the mortgage balance get that low? A couple of ways:

- Market conditions have improved since you bought the house. If you think they have improved enough, get a formal, written appraisal to prove it. Submit that to your lender.

- You have paid down the principal balance. You can do this by paying a little more than the regular principal payment on your mortgage. For instance, consider adding $50 or $100 per month to your payment. This will bring the principal down slowly. If you can afford a few hundred dollars per month, that will help.

- You have made a lump sum payment on the mortgage to bring it down to below 80 percent of the fair market value of the home. Combine that with the appraisal showing the increase in value and you may be able to save yourself $50 a month or more.

Tip #61:

Avoid PMI altogether. Don't try to handle your own mortgage application when buying a home. Find a solid, reputable loan broker to help you. Not only can they help you get the best interest rates possible, they can help you avoid paying the PMI in the first place. How? You are only required to pay the PMI if your mortgage loan is for more than 80 percent of the purchase price. A good loan broker can help you get a first mortgage for 80 percent of your purchase price and second mortgage for the rest of the loan. That way you aren't faced with any PMI costs at all. Naturally, it's a good idea to pay something down. People who didn't pay anything down ended up losing their homes when the mortgage industry collapsed. But by getting the first and second mortgages, if you can avoid the extra $50–$100 (or more) premium per month, you can use that money to pay your mortgage loan more quickly.

We have covered a wealth of details about taxes, interest, and insurance and learned a variety of special tips to help you address common problems. Let's move on to tax credits we can find around the house.

CHAPTER 6

Giving Yourself Credits around the House

A SIDE FROM BEING A great place to live, your home can provide you with a wealth of credits if you know how to go after them. The credits can come from a variety of sources, not just from the IRS.

Tip #62:

Look beyond the IRS for tax credits and rebates. Great places to look are your state, your city, your utility, and even your various appliance manufacturers. You may get access to rebates and refunds in addition to tax credits. Let's start with the simplest kind of credit.

Tip #63:

State renter's or homeowner's credits. Some states provide some kind of credit to low-income renters and/or seniors, since their rent covers a portion of the landlord's property taxes. For instance, California offers renters $60 (single or married filing separately) or $120 (all other statuses) (https://www.ftb.ca.gov/individuals/faq/ivr/203.shtml). Pennsylvania offers a property tax/rent rebate program worth up to $650 depending on your income, age, and disability level (http://www.revenue.pa.gov/generaltaxinformation/propertytaxrentrebateprogram/pages/default.aspx). To find out if your state offers anything similar, just Google "[state name] property tax credits," "[state name] renter credit," and "[state name] renter rebate." One of those searches should get you what you want. Of course, you can always go directly to your state's website to search that. Go to http://www.taxadmin.org/state-tax-agencies and look up state tax forms here: http://www.taxadmin.org/state-tax-forms.

Tip #64:

Before we look at what the IRS offers you, it's important for you to find the benefits that your state, city or utilities can provide. They can provide rebates, tax credits, or special financing. The Energy.gov site is maintained by the US Secretary of Energy and his or her staff. You can look up available benefits by selecting your state. Using this as a starting point, you can see what cost reductions you have available to you before getting to the IRS tax credits. Bear in mind you need to reduce the costs you report on any IRS or state forms by any benefits you get from these sources. In other words, if something costs you $5,000 and your utility gives you a rebate of $2,000, you will only report a cost of $3,000 to the IRS. You don't generally have to pick up the rebates as income, since you are reducing the cost of repair or improvements. Read your state's rules to find out how they want such rebates reported on their forms.

Tip #65:

Depending on your location or your income level, you might qualify for local or federal subsidy programs that will give you grant money or low-interest loans to help pay for your alternative energy devices. The White House has made renewable energy (https://www.whitehouse.gov/the-press-office/2015/08/24/fact-sheet-president-obama-announces-new-actions-bring-renewable-energy) a major goal, so you will find money flowing to communities. In particular, seek out federal funding from the PACE (property-assessed clean energy) program (http://energy.gov/eere/slsc/property-assessed-clean-energy-programs). One of the interesting things about this is that the repayment for the loan becomes part of your property tax rather than a mortgage lien on your property. The two benefits to this are that the loan balance doesn't affect your FICO score, and when you sell the house, the buyer continues to make the payment. So you get more cash out when you sell. You don't have to pay off the loan. Be sure to disclose this to all potential buyers.

Tip #66:

The Nonbusiness Energy Property Credit, Form 5695, Part II (https://www.irs.gov/pub/irs-pdf/f5695.pdf). I've seen people work themselves into a frenzy to nab this credit. This is for adding insulation to your home or replacing windows, doors, or roof components designed to reduce heat loss or gain. While doing those things might reduce your utility bill or improve the appearance of your home, the IRS tax credit for it is minimal. The entire lifetime credit amount is limited to $500 for all these improvements. (I have seen new windows costing more than $5,000.) By "lifetime," Congress means that once you have used all $500 of this credit, you may never get it again. If you are only making these improvements to get the tax benefits, think again. But do look to see if your state or utility offers any rebates.

Note: This is another of those credits that expire. This was extended through December 31, 2016, as part of the Internal Revenue Code as Section 181 of the PATH Act of 2015. Please see Bonus Tip #270 for more details.

Tip #67:

The Residential Energy Property Credit, Form 5695, Part I (https://www.irs.gov/pub/irs-pdf/f5695.pdf). This is the credit worth snagging. This gives you back 30 percent of your entire expenditure on installations of solar, geothermal, or wind energy power units and power cells. As we write this, this IRC Section 25D (https://www.law.cornell.edu/uscode/text/26/25D) credit is good for all installations paid through December 31, 2016. Naturally, the devices must meet the specifications for allowable units (https://www.energystar.gov/about/federal_tax _credits). Make sure you have all the receipts and paperwork from the contractor, including written verification that the devices meet the standards for this credit. Allowable costs include "any labor costs properly allocable to the onsite preparation, assembly, or original installation of the residential energy efficient property and for piping or wiring to interconnect such property to the home" (quoted from the instructions—that's why the wording is so stilted). Incidentally, this credit is only good on your main home or second home (like a vacation cabin), not rental property.

Tip #68:

If you are like my husband and are capable of doing your own installation of practically anything, you will undoubtedly save a lot of money. (But the job will take forever!) If you are only a master repairer in your own mind, please, be realistic and hire a professional—or your home will become "The Money Pit" (http://www.imdb.com/title/tt0091541). Never mind, let's believe you are, indeed, a master! The bad news is, the value of your labor for the installation work does not count as an installation cost. However, all the parts, supplies, and expendable tools you buy specifically for this project may be taken into account. But don't include the tools you buy that you will be able to use in the future. If you hire casual help—like those nice, convenient, inexpensive guys standing in front of Home Depot or your local hardware store—don't expect to add those costs to the installation either. In fact, don't even tell anyone about them. (A tax professional I knew hired some of those fellows to help him with his landscaping. His neighbor turned him in to California's Employment Development Department. He not only was forced to hire a licensed landscaper but faced heavy fines for hiring workers without putting them on payroll and additional fines for hiring illegal aliens. So beware of neighbors who hate you.)

Tip #69:

By hiring a professional, you will save a lot of time and money getting the installation and setup done correctly. Besides, they are also familiar with the paperwork and can answer many of your questions. Heck, they might be able to help you fill out the paperwork or give you forms that are already filled in. They might even be able to get you discounts on the materials and supplies.

Tip #70:

Most of the allowable units will have the Energy Star certification. But not all Energy Star units will qualify for the credit. The Energy Star website will help you find acceptable products, credits, and perhaps even local builders: https://www.energystar.gov.

Tip #71:

Let's do a reality check. Why do you want to install this alternative energy system in your home? Do you live off the grid or far from the nearest town? Do you live in an area where there are frequent power outages? Are your electricity bills outrageously high due to the constant need for air conditioning in the summer and heating in the winter? Then this probably makes sense. Are you a Green advocate and want to make a statement? I admire you and wonder why these alternative energy systems haven't been made a standard part of new home construction over the past fifty years.

I was in Israel in 1977 and practically every home had something that looked like a garbage can on the roof. It turned out that they were solar water heaters. We could have done that in the entire southern United States where we have sun for about two-thirds of the year—and even made the units look better. In fact, if localities had started to mandate solar, geothermal, or wind energy as appropriate to their areas, the costs of such units would have dropped dramatically by now. For instance, Iceland takes advantage of their natural resources (primarily geothermal). About 99 percent of their energy is from renewable sources, according to *Scientific American* (http://www .scientificamerican.com/article/iceland-geothermal-power).

OK, why am I wasting your time with these (to me) fascinating tidbits of information? Because I want you to think twice before you make this major expenditure for the wrong reasons. Although you might get excellent tax benefits, you will still be out-of-pocket for several thousand dollars. So please do a financial analysis of this decision. You see, my husband isn't just smart with his hands, he's also a rather practical fellow. And speaking to my interest in solar energy units, he pointed out that many of the components only last for about ten years, then need to be replaced. So when doing your financial analysis, it's important to factor in the expected life of each part of your system and the costs to replace them, as well as the costs for routine maintenance of the system. As a wife, let me add another factor. How much time does your spouse have to spend, during evenings and/or weekends doing the maintenance, if you aren't paying for the servicing? To me, the little free time we have to enjoy each other is worth more to me than saving a few bucks.

Tip #72:

Good news and bad news about this Residential Energy Credit. First the bad news—two facts:

1. When using this credit, you must reduce the basis (tax cost) of your home.
2. This is a nonrefundable credit. So if your tax liability is not high enough to use all or part of the credit, you don't get any money back at all. So you might have seriously underestimated the cost.

The good news? While the credit is not refundable, it can be carried over to the following tax year. (One year only.) Make sure you have enough income and tax liability to use up the credit. If you don't expect to have enough income, this is a good time to get an extra job; start a quick, profitable hobby; collect a bonus; or roll over retirement or IRA funds to a Roth IRA. Do some tax planning to see how the numbers balance before doing anything. And please take this into account when doing your computations.

Tip #73:

Here's a proposed cost analysis form for you to consider using:

Step A
Add all the following amounts:

1. System cost, including all components: _____

2. Permits from city, county, or local authority. _____

3. Installation costs. _____

4. Depending on the length of time to finish the installation, how much will it cost and if you need to spend any nights in a hotel or with family or friends. *Note: Staying with family or friends is never free. Factor in costs of gifts, chipping in on groceries, getting on each other's nerves, and that you will have to repay the favor at a time most inconvenient for you.* _____

5. Cost of routine maintenance and how often this must be done. (Remember, the panels need to be cleaned regularly or they lose their efficacy.) _____

6. Monthly costs (add them in × 12). _____

7. Cost of major repairs, or parts replacement and how often these need to be replaced (divide the costs by the number of years in the life of the parts). _____

8. How long you are planning to live in this house. If less than the life of the parts, divide your costs by the number of years you plan to be there to use the system. _____

9. The cost of financing. How much interest will you pay for the loan you take out to install all this? Divide the total interest you will pay over the life of the loan by the number of years the loan will run. That will give you an average annual interest cost. _____

10. Anything else that crops up (add as many lines as you need). _____

TOTAL STEP A _____

Step B

Add all the following amounts (if applicable). These are good things:

1. Rebates from your vendor or manufacturers. _____

2. Rebates from your utility companies. _____

3. Rebates from local government units. _____

4. Rebates or credits from your state. _____

5. Any other rebates or credits you get that reduce your cost. _____

6. Amount you expect to earn each year if your utility company wishes to buy your excess power to use in their grid. (Reduce whatever the system sales folk tell you by at least 50–70 percent.) _____

7. Any other goodies that come your way (use as many lines as you need). _____

TOTAL STEP B _____

Step C

Deduct the total rebates and discounts you received in **Step B** from your **Step A** costs. This will be the net cost you can use to determine your IRS energy credit.

Step D

Deduct your federal (IRS) energy credit (30 percent × **Step C**) from the net costs you arrive at in **Step C**.

This will give you your net cost for the use and installation of your new energy system after all rebates and credits. Divide this by the number of years your system is expected to last, before you have to replace most of it.

That's your annual cost.

Step E

Add up the utility bills that you realistically expect the system to replace. Review your utility bills carefully to see what it really covers. For instance, an alternative energy unit will not reduce your cost of trash pick-up, use of the sewage system, water usage, or certain other costs that may be buried in your water and power bill. It is likely to reduce cost of gas and/or propane and the need to pay for deliveries. (Did you know there were this many things you pay for in that single utility bill?) Once you determine how much you really *will* save by installing this system, compare it to the annual cost you arrived at in **Step D**.

Are you going to save any significant dollars? If it turns out that the installation will end up costing you more than you will save, you have to decide if you want to do it anyway for ecological, emotional, or other reasons. But at least you will make the decision with your eyes open. *Note: In most cases, we learned the costs were higher than the benefits.*

Step F

One last consideration to take into account if this is a financial loser. Will adding this system increase the market value of the home when you ultimately decide to sell it? If so, by how much? Alternatively, how much will it reduce the sales price of your home if the system looks ratty and shabby by the time you're ready to sell?

If you have trouble sleeping at night, consider reading these reports from the National Renewable Energy Laboratory (NREL). One is from 2009 about residential photovoltaics (http://www.nrel.gov/docs/fy10osti/46909.pdf). The other is about heating water, from 2011 (http://www.nrel.gov/docs/fy11osti/48986

.pdf). My husband is actually fascinated with this kind of material. For me? It's gibberish. Important gibberish, no doubt, but way over my head.

Tip #74:

What about leasing these systems instead of buying them? That could be a great alternative. There are lower paperwork demands, the leasing company handles the maintenance, and you just sit back and enjoy the reduced utility bills, right? You generally have to pay for the privilege. Expect to pay about $3,000 or so for them to set it up (even if they say it's free). You will not get any tax credits. They will keep them all. If this is installed on a rental property, you will not be depreciating the cost of the unit(s) because you didn't pay for them. Ask questions. If your house or property generates excess power and sends it to the grid, who gets the money—you or the solar company? If you will start paying the solar company for your utilities instead of the local utility company, what protection do you have against price increases? Read all contracts very carefully so you understand all your obligations. If you don't understand some clause—ask. Do not let them bully you or charm you away from answers. The contract will generally run for ten to twenty years. You need to make sure it is transferable to a new owner and disclose the terms to any potential buyer. Make sure you are not hampered from selling the home because of this. Find out if they will put a lien on your home, and if so, for how long? You don't want this affecting your credit. What are your obligations to maintain the roof and other adjacent parts of your home or property? For instance, if there is a tree overhanging the roof, how often do you have to trim it back (or will they)? What costs or penalties will you face if your tree damages their solar panels? Will your homeowners insurance cover this, and how much extra will it cost? Will the solar company carry insurance? What are their obligations if their installers are careless or sloppy and create roof leaks or other damage to your home? If they open up part of the roof or wall, or cut into your patio or yard, do they pay to close it up or to fix, repaint, or replant? And what if they go out of business, go bankrupt, or sell the company? Who owns your system then? Who takes care of it? So if you are considering the leasing option, be sure the company is financially solid and not planning to go public or sell their business while you live in the house (if possible).

Tip #75:

Energy credits are not limited to alternative power systems. We can also get credit for installing Energy Star appliances (https://www.energystar.gov/products/certified-products). While these credits don't come from the IRS, you can probably get them from your city, utility, or state. Generally, the stores selling these appliances can tell you all about the rebates in your area. After all, that's a powerful sales incentive. The rebates can be minor or substantial. In addition, some states have sales tax holidays that allow you to buy these appliances without paying sales taxes on certain days of the year. You can look up your state in advance so you can schedule your purchase to take advantage of that extra discount (http://www.salestaxinstitute .com/resources/sales-tax-holidays). Beware: be careful to identify specifically what you're buying and that it qualifies for the Energy Star rebate. When we bought our dishwasher at Sears several years ago, we were sure it was an Energy Star machine. After all, in the twenty-first century, who would buy an appliance that isn't? They gave us the rebate forms for the City of Los Angeles. We sent in the forms, and our credit request was rejected. Why? The specific unit Sears delivered and installed wasn't Energy Star–rated. I don't know if we received the wrong unit, but I couldn't prove this wasn't the unit we selected in the store. Avoid my error. Verify that the model and unit numbers you bought are on the paperwork with the delivered machines.

Tip #76:

Disabled access credit. This might not necessarily be a residential credit. But . . . when you run a business from home, it just might be. The credit can be as high as $5,000 (50 percent of up to $10,000 of eligible expenses). Use Form 8826 (https://www .irs.gov/pub/irs-pdf/f8826.pdf). It applies to businesses with gross receipts of less than $1,000,000 that employed no more than thirty full-time people in the past year. Most home-based businesses are likely to qualify. The expenditure can be for the purpose of removing barriers to accommodate employees, customers, clients, or the business owner. Naturally, expenditures in areas that are not used for business cannot be taken into account for this tax credit. Aside from the construction costs, here are some expenses that might surprise you (from IRC 44):

The term "eligible access expenditures" includes amounts paid or incurred—

(A) for the purpose of removing architectural, communication, physical, or transportation barriers which prevent a business from being accessible to, or usable by, individuals with disabilities,

(B) to provide qualified interpreters or other effective methods of making aurally delivered materials available to individuals with hearing impairments,

(C) to provide qualified readers, taped texts, and other effective methods of making visually delivered materials available to individuals with visual impairments,

(D) to acquire or modify equipment or devices for individuals with disabilities, or

(E) to provide other similar services, modifications, materials, or equipment (https://www.law.cornell.edu/ uscode/text/26/44).

Incidentally, this only applies to modifications to existing buildings. Expenditures for new construction do not qualify.

Tip #77:

Disabled access deduction. While this isn't a credit, it is a tax break. These costs might be useful as *medical deductions*. Sometimes it is necessary to make modifications to entrances, hallways, bathrooms, bedrooms, and even the patio area to make the home accessible for someone with physical disabilities. The adjustments may be minor, like adding handholds to bathtubs, showers, and certain walls. Or they may be extensive, like remodeling rooms, making doors wider, putting moulding or railings on walls as handholds, installing ramps, or installing special pools or spa systems. Be sure to get paperwork from the physician spelling out what improvements are needed and why. Without a physician's order, you will not be able to claim any medical deductions. Keep copies of all the receipts in a permanent file as well as the tax file for the year the improvements were made. The deduction is a little tricky, especially if the costs are high. The IRS has a worksheet in Publication 502 to help you (https://www.irs.gov/publications/p502/ar02.html). You may only deduct the costs to the extent that they did not increase the value of the home. So if there is a lot of money at stake (like tens of thousands of dollars), it's worth the investment to get a professional appraisal on the home—before the improvements and afterwards—to be able to prove how much the value increased, if at all. Remember, not all improvements increase a home's worth. In fact, some modifications might be downright annoying to people who don't have disabilities.

CHAPTER 7

Extra Income around the House

THESE DAYS, PEOPLE ARE still hurting. Mortgage payments rose after the first year or two of low, teaser payments. Long-term, high-paying jobs were lost. They were often replaced by jobs paying substantially less. And, sadly, the financial stresses caused divorces.

Several years ago, my hairdresser told me that she was getting a divorce and would have to sell their home. After all, Rita couldn't afford the mortgage payment on her own. Listening to her lament, I realized things were even worse than that. Since the economy was in bad shape at the time, home values had dropped dramatically. In order to sell the house (whose value had dropped to about $150,000), she would have to contribute about $3,000 of her own money to make the sale work, since her mortgage was higher than the market value. (Yes, we're just recovering from another cycle like that.) If you are smart and creative, there is never a reason to lose your home. Here are several ways to put your home to work for you so it pays for itself . . . and more.

Tip #78:

A solution for someone who is unable to afford the mortgage: the more she told me about her house, with the pool and the large, charming backyard, the more I realized it was a pretty valuable property. Rita needed to keep that house. I advised her not to sell, to get her husband to sign a release to any future claim to this property, and to get a roommate. With someone paying rent and a share of the utilities, Rita could afford to keep the house. That's exactly what she did. To free up some additional cash, Rita stopped paying rent in a salon and converted her patio into a salon. That helped cut her cash outflow. The value of that house has risen to nearly $600,000 from the $150,000 it was worth during her divorce. This same strategy can work for other divorced folks and even for couples. It might require sacrificing a little space. Be very, very careful about screening the roommate—for both financial stability and compatible personality (and noise-level preferences). Do not rent to family or friends. They are apt to skip payments when convenient. And it's hard to kick them out—on so many levels. Besides, you might end up losing the friend or alienating the family member and other family members, as you end up being the villain when they don't pay you.

Tip #79:

A 14-day rental loophole: speaking of just needing some cash to supplement your budget, did you know that you could rent your home or vacation property for up to 14 days each year without reporting any of that income (https://

**www.irs.gov/publications/p527/ch05.html#en_US_2014
_publink1000219202)?** Yup. This is perfect for time-shares
you can't really afford to use right now. Depending on your
home, you can probably rent the property for $100–$300 or
more per night depending on the configuration of the property
and the number of people. That's worth $1,400–$4,200, tax-free.
You don't get to deduct any of the costs. After all, you're not
reporting any income. Beware: rent the property for 15 days or
more overall during the year and all the income becomes taxable. *Note: Check to see if your state follows this rule. Most do.*

Tip #80:

Film location. Does your home or property have some interesting or unique quality that might make it attractive to a film
company? Consider listing it with a service used by location
managers. California, where many films are shot, has a State
Film Commission website where you can find reliable places to
list your home (http://www.film.ca.gov/How_to_Market.htm).
New York City's mayor's office offers a way to "make your home
a star" (http://www.nyc.gov/html/film/html/for_residents/star
.shtml). A recent venture from the AirBnB folks called Peer-
Space is also designed for film location scouts and business
location scouts (http://techcrunch.com/2014/09/17/peerspace).
So far, they are just in New York and California (https://www
.peerspace.com). But you know their locations will be expanded.
Many other states and Canada are becoming more attractive
for film production. Googling turned up several other services,
but I couldn't find any evidence that they had successfully helped
people get their homes rented. So search your state's website to
see if your state offers a directory, which will list reputable location services. Incidentally, my brother's very ordinary home
was used for filming. They repaired his ten-foot glass patio door,
replaced his worn-out rug, and made some other repairs, since

they had the tools and materials handy. So your home doesn't have to be fancy or unique to be useful to a production company. What are the advantages? Here are just a few:

- High compensation. You might get more than $1,000 per day. All of it is taxable.

- Permanent improvements to your home—like new carpeting or drapes, repairs, and certain upgrades—at no charge to you. These repairs don't constitute taxable income, since they are tenant repairs or improvements. *Note: Some things are just brought in for the film and removed when they leave, like plants, furniture, accessories.*

- Short-term usage of the property. For a couple of weeks' use, you might earn enough money to pay your mortgage for a year. Several people I have known over the years have earned more than $50,000 in a month or less this way and have gotten some nice improvements to their home.

Tip #81:

General short-term rental thoughts. Let me tell you a little story. Once upon a time, my friend Layne Neugart (http://articles .hbindependent.com/2001-07-26/news/export9180_1_fourth -of-july-parade-parade-west-grand-marshal) used to lead the annual Huntington Beach Fourth of July parade, flanked by Boy Scouts and his personal American flag. Layne started a business to cater to visitors at the 1984 Summer Olympic Games (http:// www.olympic.org/los-angeles-1984-summer-olympics) held in Los Angeles, after seeing news reports warning that there would not be enough hotel rooms to accommodate the flood of visitors. Clearly, personal residences would be needed. Starting two years before the Olympic Games, Layne, his staff, and I worked out the details to safely rent out a personal residence—protecting both the homeowner and the visitor from damage, fraud, theft, and so on. We urged him to get a real estate license. That turned out to be a great idea. You see, the state of California decided there were too many phony "Olympic Rental Services" and limited the market to only licensed real estate agents and brokers. We arranged for low-cost insurance, either per rental or long term. We arranged for a maid service to clean the places before and after each visitor. Since this was still in the days of landline phones, we built in protections against visitors running up long-distance charges. Today, that's not an issue. People carry their own cell phones or can get them at CVS or 7-11 for short-term visits. We created a portfolio containing both elegant estates and quite ordinary homes along the Southern California coastline from Oxnard to San Diego. Some people rented out rooms and hosted their visitors. Others rented out the entire home and went on vacation. After all, the lure of two weeks of tax-free rental income was tantalizing. For some homeowners, this was the first real vacation they got to take in years. This venture was such a success that people from all over the world, including sheiks, other royalty, and just plain folks continued to use his service to visit California until Layne died eight years after our Los Angeles Olympic Summer.

What's the point? Based on what we learned, if you're going to rent your home out for a week here, another week there, particularly as an absentee landlord, you need to take sensible precautions. Even more so if you have a home or property that you want to rent out full time.

- Turn off your landline phone service. Let people use their cell phones. If they don't have them for here in the United States, point them to the nearest 7–11 or local store where they can get cheap, use-based cell phones for short-term use. *Note: Simply removing the phone from the plug won't prevent someone from plugging in another phone.*

- Turn off all pay-per-view features on your cable or satellite system.

- Remove all computers that contain *any* personal information or passwords. Consider leaving an inexpensive computer there just for visitors to use.

- Do you have personal items that are special to you, especially family pictures and such, that are not easy to replace? Either lock them away safely or take good scans of them so you can reproduce them if they are inadvertently lost, misplaced, or destroyed. Naturally, any jewelry, furniture, or knickknacks of value should be removed from the home entirely.

- Stop your mail. You don't want strangers snooping through your mail, getting your checks, opening your credit card offers, getting your replacement credit cards, or potentially stealing your identity. In fact, if you are going to rent your home out frequently, get yourself a PO Box service— preferably not from the US Postal Service. Why? Because with private services, you can call them up, reach a live person quickly and easily, and have them tell you what mail has arrived. If you made prior arrangements, perhaps they can even open and scan your time-sensitive mail for you. However, if you have newspaper delivery, let that continue. Your guests will enjoy the local news and information about local events, attractions, films, television schedules, and so on.

- If you have pets and will be leaving them in your home, you must absolutely vet your guest in advance. To some, having your pet stay home is an added attraction. But you don't want them to neglect to feed your pet, harm your pet, or steal your pet.

- Folks with pools should consider not renting to anyone with children. If you do rent to families with children, make sure you have a strong fence around the pool—one that cannot be climbed over by small children—and be sure to put a solid lock on the fence. Have the parents sign a statement when they get that key, agreeing that they will be with the children and watching them at all times when they use the pool.

- If you are leaving town, make sure that you have a reliable local friend or associate drop by and check on the visitors. They should have a key to the place. The visitors should be informed this person will be dropping by to make sure they find everything they need, or to see if they need help operating washing machines, dishwashers, cable televisions, and so on.

- Make sure your contract includes a provision to get reimbursed for stolen linens or other personal items. A reasonable security deposit would work. In this case, make sure you provide an inventory of all key items that the visitor can sign when they arrive. The same number of towels, linens, and so on should be there when they leave.

- If you install cameras so you can look in on your place remotely, be sure to tell your guests in advance, in the listing. Show them how to turn off the cameras so they have privacy.

- Check the rental laws with your city, community association (if you have one), and so on. At what point do you have to register and collect/pay hotel taxes? After a certain number of days, a certain level of income, or what? Legitimate hotels and bed and breakfast locations are screaming about the lack of registration by online hosts. New laws are being considered or passed to require hosts to pay fees like all other hostelries. See also http://www.nytimes.com/roomfordebate/2015/06/16/san-francisco-and-new-york-weigh-airbnbs-effect-on-rent/airbnb-is-a-problem-for-cities-like-new-york-and-san-francisco. In addition, "In a three-year study published last year, New York State Attorney General Eric Schneiderman found that 72 percent of AirBnB listings are for

illegal rentals" (http://mashable.com/2015/07/15/short-term
-rentals-lobbying/#3m2mff5fMgqn).

All these costs that are specifically related to your rental activities will be deductible. Of course, the question is: Where on
your tax return will you be reporting this income?

Tip #82:

AirBnB rentals. They have become quite the craze. Over the
years there have been other sites, worldwide, making it possible
for people to list their homes, rooms, vacation properties, and
so on for rent to strangers without the need for rental agents to
act as intermediaries. But AirBnB has become one of the top
markets (https://www.airbnb.com). One of the attractive features of the service is that they don't charge any fees to list your
property. You only pay them when they get you a paying guest.
OK, so they are giving you money. How do you report the income from AirBnB and any other rental sources? You have three
different ways to handle the income. You may be able to decide
whether to use option 1 or 2. When it comes to option 3, even
if you don't select it, the IRS might—in an audit. So I'll give you
some tips on how to avoid that problem. Let's explore the differences among the following options:

1. As regular residential real estate rentals on Schedule E

2. As hotel-type rentals on Schedule C

3. As casual rentals, not rented for profit

Note 1: AirBnB does not post a phone number on their contact page or anywhere on their website. Although their
   Twitter team recommended that I email their press office, the press office did not respond, despite repeated
   requests and alerts that I was working on deadline. As

a result, I am not able to provide you with the specifics about how they handle their income reporting to you, their management of long-term rentals, or other key information I had hoped to provide for you. The fact that they were so unresponsive might be a concern when you place your properties and trust in their hands.

Note 2: Both visitors and hosts have had problems reaching AirBnB according to the Better Business Bureau and PissedConsumer.com (http://www.bbb.org/greater-san-francisco/business-reviews/rental-vacancy-listing-service/airbnb-in-san-francisco-ca-375521/complaints; http://airbnb.pissedconsumer.com). However, based on the volume of activity in the AirBnB system, the percentage of problems does seem to be quite low. Regardless, *do* look up your potential host's track record before booking. And if they accept reviews about guests, look up your guest before renting to a stranger.

Tip #83:

Residential rental. What are the considerations for treating vacation traveler rental income as Schedule E rentals (https://www.irs.gov/pub/irs-pdf/f1040se.pdf)? Read IRS Publication 527 for in-depth information about rentals (https://www.irs.gov/publications/p527). Typically, Schedule E is used to report income from long-term rentals—in other words, income from tenants who move in and stay more than a month at a time. When you have a long-term tenant, someone who signs a lease and lives in the room or the home for a year or more, Schedule E is the way to go. The IRS considers this passive income. There are all kinds of special limits when it comes to deducting losses. (Congress simplified the US Internal Revenue Code with the Tax Reform Act of 1986. Whew! That was a killer.) We'll talk more about expenses shortly in Tip #88. Meanwhile, consider reading IRS Publication 925 about Passive Losses (https://www.irs.gov/publications/p925/index.html). The advantage to using Schedule E comes into play when your rentals are profitable. Although you pay income taxes on the profits, you don't pay the self-employment taxes of 15.3 percent on the profits. The problems and complications arise when you have losses. In fact, owning rental property will probably be an entire book all by itself. There are so many complicated rules, nuances, and traps, they could fill volumes.

Tip #84:

Hotel-type rentals. These are short-term rentals generally reported on your Schedule C, like a business (https://www.irs.gov/pub/irs-pdf/f1040sc.pdf). Tenants typically stay for a few days, or a week or two. (Some tax professionals treat this as a Schedule E, passive rental, regardless. The decision will be on a case-by-case basis.) In addition, it's important to learn your locality's definition of a hotel. (For instance, in the City of Los Angeles, the Transient Occupancy Tax applies to any rental for thirty consecutive calendar days or less: http://finance.lacity.org/Content/TaxInfoBooklet.htm.) Be sure to look up your city's rules to determine if you are subject to the hotel taxes and rules. Incidentally, it's not just potential taxes and licensing fees you might face. There may also be zoning prohibitions against short-term rentals. Folks who live in a community with CC&Rs (Covenants, Conditions, and Restrictions) might have to get written clearance from the homeowners' association board of directors. When it comes to tax issues, the bad news is you pay income taxes *and* self-employment taxes of 15.3 percent on the profits, if your activities are considered hotel-like. The good news is, if you have profits, these profits will count as earned income in case you want to make contributions to your IRA or other retirement plan. And when you have legitimate losses, there is no limit to the losses you can deduct (except for office in home deductions).

And when you have losses, those losses will reduce your AGI without being limited by the Alternative Minimum Tax.

Tip #85:

And then there are the casual rentals, not rented for profit. Often, this revenue comes from renting at deep discounts to family or friends, renting out rooms for extremely low fees, or just renting the house or rooms out if someone happens to ask, with no active attempt to try to attract paying guests. Avoid finding yourself in this last category. This is the worst of all worlds. You must report all the income on line 21 of your Form 1040 (the Other Income line), but your deductions face several limits. The first of which is that you may only deduct your expenses up to the amount of your gross rental income. Then you must report the expenses on Schedule A as Miscellaneous Itemized Deductions, which means you must itemize. If you own a home with a mortgage, you're probably already using Schedule A, so that may not be a major obstacle. But the deductions are reduced by 2 percent of your AGI. And if your income is really high, your itemized deductions might be limited by the Alternative Minimum Taxes (AMT) and the itemized deduction phaseout. Often, you will only get the benefit of half of your expenses or less.

Tip #86:

Proving that your rentals really are for profit. This is especially important in two circumstances:

1. When your Schedule E or Schedule C for your rental activities show losses consistently for more than a couple of years.

2. When you end up with very few days of paying visitors during a given year. If this is the case, how can you prove your intention to make a profit? One of the best ways is

to list your rental everywhere you possibly can, including a Facebook page, Twitter account, your own website, and perhaps make some videos to put on YouTube. For example, take a look at Paradise Regained in Utila, Honduras (http://www.paradiseregainedutila.com). See how many places it's listed (https://www.google.com/search?q =paradise+honduras&ie=utf-8&oe=utf-8"\l"q=paradise +regained+utila+honduras&start=10)? CrunchBase.com shows some competitors to help you start your research (https://www.crunchbase.com/organization/airbnb/ competitors). Try to take care not to list your place somewhere with a bad reputation to avoid being swindled or worse. (This is totally unofficial, but Craigslist scares me. It's like the old Wild West—wide open with no sheriff.) Another suggestion is to keep really good records of all people who called to rent and what the disposition was of each query. After all, no one closes 100 percent of their potential sales opportunities. Sometimes the time, availability, or amenities won't suit them. Sometimes you will have legitimate objections and won't accept the potential visitor or tenant. Or your area may become undesirable for a while due to storms, earthquakes, sudden local violence—whatever the reason for not being able to rent your place, keep records and document that you tried to get tenants. In addition, create a business plan—a plan that describes steps you plan to take to attract tenants. Use that as a checklist throughout the year, showing what steps you have taken each month. The goal is to prove that you have a profit motive and are not just sporadically renting out your home. Incidentally, if you do set up a business plan and use it, you will not only outwit the IRS, but actually make more money than you can ever imagine!

Tip #87:

Incidentally, when it comes to working with companies like AirBnB, follow their guidelines. When they tell you not to accept payment outside their system, don't think you're putting one over on them by pocketing money without paying them their fee. By bypassing their rules, you will have cost yourself all protection related to that guest (and perhaps get booted out). If that guest does damage, you will have to handle the conflict yourself. They won't be there to intervene for you.

Tip #88:

Deduct it all. Renting out your home gives you an excellent opportunity to deduct everything. The smart Tax Vigilante will track every itty bitty receipt and detail about every possible expenditure. The great thing about this obsessiveness is that you present your tax professional with all your costs. The tax pro can review them and decide what is and what is not deductible. Often, because a client has tracked every detail, I will notice valid deductible expenditures that he or she might not have thought to show me on their own. Not everyone has the patience for all that record keeping. So at least be Tax Aware and track as many of your expenses as possible. Naturally, you can fully deduct all costs for expenses directly related to the photographing, displaying, advertising, and management of the rentals. But on the Schedule E or Schedule C of your tax return, you will be able to deduct the business-use percentage of many of your costs that don't change very much when tenants move in—long or short term. What things can you deduct that you spend money on anyway? See the following four lists.

1. Costs you can fully deduct now but can move to Schedule E or C to reduce your Adjusted Gross Income (AGI) and/ or your self-employment taxes:

   • Mortgage interest

- Property taxes
- Mortgage insurance premiums

2. Costs you pay every month but never get a deduction for because the IRS considers them personal expenses:
   - Community Association fees
   - Gardener
   - Homeowner's insurance
   - Pool fellow
   - Utilities (except the ones you've turned off while you have paying guests)
   - Newspapers

3. Costs you pay especially because you have guests or to attract a higher class of guest but that might benefit you anyway:
   - Housecleaning
   - Groceries and goodies bought specifically to welcome guests
   - New towels and linens
   - New carpets or drapes
   - Wide-screen television
   - Shiny new dishes and cutlery
   - Other stuff you bought to make the place appealing—to "stage" the photos and the experience

4. And there's a cost you don't pay at all but can be a substantial deduction—depreciation.

Tip #89:

Depreciation. This is a phantom deduction for the wear and tear of the home due to business use. You don't actually spend any money on it for tax purposes. In reality, the idea was for people to put some money in reserve each year to repair and replace things that tend to wear out, like roofs, driveways, plumbing, walls that need cleaning and painting, carpets and drapes that need replacing, and so on. That concept has been forgotten, but the deduction stays behind. How do you depreciate your home? Well, you need to know your tax basis in your home (please see the glossary). You also need to know the breakdown between the value of the building and the land. You may not depreciate the land—just the building. Warning: if the value of your home has declined since you bought it, you will be using the fair market value instead of the tax basis. Frankly, when it comes to setting up the correct values for depreciation, go see a tax pro. You should not be doing this yourself. Get a worksheet on this with the backup data and documentation that was used to establish the correct depreciation schedule. With that, you might be able to do this yourself in future years. If you live in a condominium or co-op, you don't really own any land directly, but you do own a share of the overall land that belongs to your community. So don't think there is no land value. There is.

Assuming you will be renting out your entire place to each set of guests, you will use the following ratio for depreciation:

1. Start with the building's basis or the lower fair market value of the building only (not the land)

2. Multiply that by the number of days rented divided by 365 days (366 days in 2016, a Leap Year) =

3. The percentage of rental use

Table A-6. Residential Rental Property
            Mid-Month Convention
            Straight Line—27.5 Years

Year	Month property placed in service											
	1	2	3	4	5	6	7	8	9	10	11	12
1	3.485%	3.182%	2.879%	2.576%	2.273%	1.970%	1.667%	1.364%	1.061%	0.758%	0.455%	0.152%
2–9	3.636	3.636	3.636	3.636	3.636	3.636	3.636	3.636	3.636	3.636	3.636	3.636
10	3.637	3.637	3.637	3.637	3.637	3.637	3.636	3.636	3.636	3.636	3.636	3.636
11	3.636	3.636	3.636	3.636	3.636	3.636	3.637	3.637	3.637	3.637	3.637	3.637
12	3.637	3.637	3.637	3.637	3.637	3.637	3.636	3.636	3.636	3.636	3.636	3.636
13	3.636	3.636	3.636	3.636	3.636	3.636	3.637	3.637	3.637	3.637	3.637	3.637
14	3.637	3.637	3.637	3.637	3.637	3.637	3.636	3.636	3.636	3.636	3.636	3.636
15	3.636	3.636	3.636	3.636	3.636	3.636	3.637	3.637	3.637	3.637	3.637	3.637
16	3.637	3.637	3.637	3.637	3.637	3.637	3.636	3.636	3.636	3.636	3.636	3.636
17	3.636	3.636	3.636	3.636	3.636	3.636	3.637	3.637	3.637	3.637	3.637	3.637
18	3.637	3.637	3.637	3.637	3.637	3.637	3.636	3.636	3.636	3.636	3.636	3.636
19	3.636	3.636	3.636	3.636	3.636	3.636	3.637	3.637	3.637	3.637	3.637	3.637
20	3.637	3.637	3.637	3.637	3.637	3.637	3.636	3.636	3.636	3.636	3.636	3.636
21	3.636	3.636	3.636	3.636	3.636	3.636	3.637	3.637	3.637	3.637	3.637	3.637
22	3.637	3.637	3.637	3.637	3.637	3.637	3.636	3.636	3.636	3.636	3.636	3.636
23	3.636	3.636	3.636	3.636	3.636	3.636	3.637	3.637	3.637	3.637	3.637	3.637
24	3.637	3.637	3.637	3.637	3.637	3.637	3.636	3.636	3.636	3.636	3.636	3.636
25	3.636	3.636	3.636	3.636	3.636	3.636	3.637	3.637	3.637	3.637	3.637	3.637
26	3.637	3.637	3.637	3.637	3.637	3.637	3.636	3.636	3.636	3.636	3.636	3.636
27	3.636	3.636	3.636	3.636	3.636	3.636	3.637	3.637	3.637	3.637	3.637	3.637
28	1.97	2.273	2.576	2.879	3.182	3.485	3.636	3.636	3.636	3.636	3.636	3.636
29							0.152	0.455	0.758	1.061	1.364	1.667

If you are only renting out some rooms and you're staying there, it gets more complicated because you will have to take the rented area into account. Definitely get a tax pro to help you!

IRS Publication 946 explains depreciation and provides the tables and number of years to use for various assets (https://www.irs.gov/publications/p946). When it comes to renting your home, you will use the residential real estate life of 27.5 years. See IRS Table A-6, above: https://www.irs.gov/publications/p946/ar02.html.

Note: There are a variety of permanent changes to depreciation deduction rules in the Internal Revenue Code as Part 3 of the PATH Act of 2015. Please see Bonus Tip #270 for more details.

Tip #90:

Pet hosting. You're not a people lover. Don't want them in your house? How about dogs or cats? More than 43 million households have dogs living within. 36 million homes are ruled by cats (https://www.avma.org/KB/Resources/Statistics/Pages/Market-research-statistics-US-pet-ownership.aspx). Where do all these animals stay when their parents are at work or away on a trip? Pet care places are popping up all over the country, from commercial places like PetSmart to high-end salons. These offer much better and more personalized care than old-fashioned kennels seem to, where animals are simply held in cages and fed on a schedule. But why am I telling you? You can join the fun, too, by signing up as a pet-sitter for DogVacay (https://dogvacay .com/how-it-works). It's almost like a dating service for pet fanciers. (After all, Jennifer Lopez's character, Charlie, struck gold as a dog-walker in *Monster-in-Law*—it could happen to you, too.) You get to meet the pet(s) and owners before agreeing to care for the animals, before they reluctantly relinquish care of their dearly beloved family member to you. You get to decide how many pets you will accept for a single day, overnight, or multiple-day stay. It's a great way to earn extra money without leaving the house. You don't need a college degree or specialized skills. Just patience, attention to detail, and an honest-to-goodness affection for the animals in your care. It doesn't hurt to get some specialized training, which DogVacay provides. The company provides insurance coverage, a 24/7 emergency phone number in case you need help, and helps you negotiate costs when their pet causes damage to your home.

Tip #91:

Income from pet care. Naturally, you report all your income as business income on Schedule C. Their position is that they are actually acting as your banker and collecting the credit card payments. They send you the money, less their fees. So you will get a Form 1099-K from DogVacay, not a Form 1099-MISC (https:// www.irs.gov/pub/irs-pdf/f1099k.pdf). They only issue that form if you have had more than two hundred transactions or earned $20,000 or more. The amount shown will only be the net amount that you receive after DogVacay takes its cut. So if you don't meet that level of income or transactions, it's important for you to maintain your own income records. Most likely, you will be able to look up a summary of your transactions online. Just in case, it's wise to record or download the data into your accounting system.

Tip #92:

Tracking doggy-kitty daycare direct costs. The actual costs of the animal's food and supplies should be relatively easy to track. When shopping for groceries, the smart way to separate the cost of personal groceries from pet guest groceries is to separate them on the checkout conveyor belt. Just put that little plastic spacer between your groceries and the guest's supplies. In fact, it would also be smart to use a separate check, debit card, or credit card. Using the separate bank account or credit card to pay for business-related expenses makes it easier to track them.

Tip #93:

Pet daycare office in your home. With animals running around your entire home and yard, how do you determine your office-in-home-type costs? First of all, you will take into account all the expenses we discussed in Tip #88. Again, this is a good time to speak to your tax pro about how to get the maximum depreciation deduction. But if you want a guideline for how to handle this, read the IRS depreciation explanation for day care facilities in Publication 587 (https://www.irs.gov/publications/p587/ar02 .html). Your issues are essentially the same as if you were providing care for children or seniors, except that the special food and meal tables they describe won't apply to dogs and cats. You will have a special area on Form 8829, the Office in Home form, to enter both the square footage of your home and the number of hours it was used for day (or night) care. See the top of Form 8829: https://www.irs.gov/pub/irs-pdf/f8829.pdf.

Part I	Part of Your Home Used for Business			
1	Area used regularly and exclusively for business, regularly for daycare, or for storage of inventory or product samples (see instructions)	1		
2	Total area of home	2		
3	Divide line 1 by line 2. Enter the result as a percentage	3		%
	For daycare facilities not used exclusively for business, go to line 4. All others, go to line 7.			
4	Multiply days used for daycare during year by hours used per day	4	hr.	
5	Total hours available for use during the year (365 days x 24 hours) (see instructions)	5	8,760 hr.	
6	Divide line 4 by line 5. Enter the result as a decimal amount . . .	6	.	
7	Business percentage. For daycare facilities not used exclusively for business, multiply line 6 by line 3 (enter the result as a percentage). All others, enter the amount from line 3 . . . . . ▶	7		%

Tip #94:

Paying for services. Generally, when a business pays an individual who provides services or rental facilities $600 or more in any year, we must issue a Form 1099-MISC to that freelance worker by January 31 of the following year. If you've ever tried to get their Social Security number in January, you may have been faced with a variety of unproductive reactions. They range from complete indifference (ignoring your request), to hostility, to outright violence. You might be surprised to learn how many people have no intention of reporting what you pay them—and become infuriated when you tell them, after the year is over, that you are reporting their income to the IRS. You can avoid this problem by having the service provider give you a filled out and signed Form W-9 before you hire them—and certainly before you issue the first check (https://www.irs.gov/pub/irs-pdf/fw9.pdf). (TaxMama recommends getting this form signed even before you pay them anywhere close to $600. Once you like a person's services, the dollars add up. Pretty soon they have earned more than $600 and you can ruin a beautiful relationship by springing this on them in the middle of the year.) Making it clear that you need this form from them upfront means they know they will be paying taxes on this stream of income. They can factor the taxes into their fee for the services they provide to you. You will need this from the housekeepers, repair folks, gardeners, and other people who have been providing services to you for years without ever being 1099'd. That may cause a bit of a stir.

Several years ago, Congress was playing around with the 1099-MISC rules and rescinded the rule requiring rental property owners who report their rentals on Schedule E to issue 1099-MISCs. However, some tax professionals still insist on it. And if you're reporting your rental income on Schedule C, you must issue the 1099-MISC to all service providers to whom you pay $600 or more during the year.

Tip #95:

Filing the 1099-MISC. Not filing carries a penalty of $250, or 10 percent of the total amounts on all 1099-MISCs that should have been filed (https://www.irs.gov/irm/part4/irm _04-023-009.html). *Note: Section 806 of the Trade Preferences Extension Act of 2015 just raised the penalty to $250 from $100* (https://www.congress.gov/bill/114th-congress/ house-bill/1295/text/pl). It's best to file these forms online. You can use the IRS's service. It's called FIRE (Filing Information Returns Electronically; https://www.irs.gov/Tax-Professionals/ e-File-Providers-%26-Partners/Filing-Information-Returns -Electronically-%28FIRE%29). There are also several inexpensive services that can do this for you. For instance, Intuit Payroll will file them and send copies to the freelancers for under $20 for up to three 1099s.

Tip #96:

Want to avoid filing the 1099-MISC altogether? All you need to do is pay all your service providers by credit card or by PayPal. If you do that, the credit card company or PayPal will send them a 1099-K and you're off the hook (https://www.irs.gov/uac/ General-FAQs-on-New-Payment-Card-Reporting-Requirements)!

If transactions are already reportable on other information returns, must they be reported again by payment settlement entities? No. If a transaction is reportable by a PSE both under section 6041 or section 6041 A(a) and under section 6050W, the transaction must be reported on a Form 1099-K and not a Form 1099-MISC.

CHAPTER 8

In the Garage

THESE DAYS EACH HOME has at least one car (and several televisions or other viewing devices). Some people are sharing the single car, driving each other to work. Others have multiple cars. Sadly, we fall into the latter category. Our driveway is filled with four vehicles at all times, plus one parked in the front of the house. At least two of them run. The rest? Only sometimes. The MGB? It will run again, someday. Sigh . . .

One of the things that has always puzzled me about auto insurance rates is this: Why must we pay full, separate fees for each and every car when there are only two people driving? After all, we can only drive one car at a time. Why aren't we charged for the number of drivers, the highest replacement value (collision) for the most expensive vehicle, and our choice of liability coverage? Oh well, you figure it out.

Tip #97:

One of the most common sources of tax breaks comes from the use of vehicles. There are four ways to take advantage of vehicle-related deductions:

1. Charitable mileage
2. Medical mileage
3. Moving mileage
4. Business or job-related mileage

Tip #98:

Charitable mileage. This comes in at 14 cents per mile. The mileage rate is set by Congress, so it has not changed since 1998. (In 1997 it was 12 cents per mile.) Keep track of all charity-related driving. That includes going to meetings, volunteer work, driving your charitable charges to doctors' offices, meetings, events, campgrounds, and so on.

Tip #99:

Charitable parking. Be sure to track all parking costs. If you don't get a receipt (due to meters or other mechanical payments), write a note with the date, time, and amount of the parking fee and the charitable purpose.

Tip #100:

Business, moving, and medical mileage rates change annually. For 2015, the rates were:

- business—57.5 cents per mile
- moving and medical—23 cents per mile

For 2016, the rates are:

- business—54 cents per mile
- moving and medical—19 cents per mile

The IRS computes the new rates based on cost of living increases and some other factors. Generally, the rates only change in January. However, in years when gas prices rise or drop dramatically, the rates may change two or three times during the year. Most recently, in 2008 and 2011, we had two rates. You can look up the most current mileage rates and the history since 1997 on this IRS page: http://www.irs.gov/Tax-Professionals/Standard-Mileage-Rates.

Just in case the IRS changes the page's URL, this page on the Small Business & Management website is consistently available: http://www.smbiz.com/sbrl003.html#smr.

Tip #101:

Make a note of the mileage shown on your vehicle(s) odometer(s) as early as possible in the beginning of the year so you have the starting point to track your annual mileage. Remember to write down the mileage at the end of year. You will need to know the total miles driven on each car each year when you deduct mileage for anything. If you didn't start January out with this annual tradition, you can work backward to extrapolate the mileage in six easy steps:

1. Find a service or tune-up receipt for each car from the earliest date this year, or the latest date last year. It will show the mileage at the time of the service. Write that down.

2. Write down the mileage on your odometer today. Subtract the earlier mileage from today's mileage. Pretend the mileage on January 18 was 56,117 and the mileage today is 58,326—the difference is 2,209 miles.

3. Count the number of days between the two dates. Suppose the service was done on January 18 and today is February 26, making it 39 days.

4. Divide the miles you've driven by the number of days. 2,209 divided by 39 = 56.64 miles per day.

5. Multiply the daily mileage by the number of days in the year so far. For example, if you are doing this on February 26, there have been 57 days so far this year = 3,228 miles driven this year.

6. Subtract the result from today's odometer reading to get the beginning mileage for the year. Voila! 58,326 minus 3,228 = 55,098 is your approximate mileage on January 1.

Tip #102:

Track your moving mileage. That's pretty easy. You generally won't be doing this more than once a year. In order to deduct moving expenses at all you must meet the distance test: "Your new main job location is at least fifty miles farther from your former home than your old main job location was from your former home" (https://www.irs.gov/publications/p521/ar02.html). What mileage counts? Only the mileage you drive to move your household to the new location. If you are driving several cars (yours, your spouse's, your teens, etc.) record the mileage on each car—and identify the car for the tax records. You may not use the mileage to drive to the new location to scout out a new home, or a job, or anything else. Just the pure moving-related mileage. However, if you rent a moving van, no need to worry about mileage. (Though keep the receipt because that is excellent proof of the distance driven.) When using a moving van, you deduct the cost of the rental and the fuel you bought throughout the trip—including the last fuel fill-up before you returned the rental car. Deduct all your moving expenses on Form 3903 (https://www.irs.gov/pub/irs-pdf/f3903.pdf). This will carry the allowable deduction to the front page of your Form 1040. You will be able to use these expenses even if you cannot itemize.

Tip #103:

More about moving. As long as we're talking about moving mileage, let's outline some of the other moving costs that are deductible. Naturally, if you pay a moving and storage company to move all your goods, you can deduct the full amount you pay them. Deduct your travel expenses—hotels, motels, or campgrounds along the way—for yourself and your moving helpers. Incidentally, be aware that someone might break into your rented moving conveyance. Please take appropriate precautions and keep irreplaceable valuables with you at all times.

Tip #104:

Moving insurance. Beware of theft. I have heard of several instances where people woke up and found that that the lock on their moving vehicle had been broken and many of their possessions had been stolen or ransacked. Or that their moving vehicle had been stolen outright. Stay in places where there is security or someone on the lodging's desk at night. Try to get a room where the desk clerk can see your room and your car. Get moving insurance—the cost will be deductible. Ask your present homeowners insurance agent for information about a policy, or search online for moving insurance. If you are working with a moving and storage company, it helps to understand their terminology and what your coverage does and doesn't offer. About.com

has a page with good definitions (http://moving.about.com/od/
hiringamovingcompany/tp/Definition-Of-Moving-Insurance
-Terms-You-Should-Know.htm).

Tip #105:

Moving costs you may not deduct. There is no deduction for
meals. Not yours, not your moving companions. If you don't
drive directly from your old home to your new home, there is
no mileage deduction for side trips and touring around while
making the move. So if you have taken this travel opportunity
to indulge your curiosity, print out a Google Maps or MapQuest
page showing what the direct mileage would have been. Store it
in your tax file for the year.

Tip #106:

Reimbursements. Lots of large or wealthy employers provide full
reimbursements for all your moving expenses. In fact, if you're lucky,
some employers even reimburse you for the costs of selling your
old residence and buying your new one. Doesn't that feel amazing?
The bad news is most of those reimbursements are taxable income,
since they are far beyond the actual deductible moving costs. The
good news is those extra reimbursements have already been added
to your wages and withholding has been taken. It would be wise to
review your overall income with a tax pro in the year of your move
to make sure you have had enough taxes withheld to cover the extra
income. On the other hand, if you have only been reimbursed for
moving and mileage, it's not added to your income and you don't
need to report anything on your tax return. On the third hand (do
you have three hands?), you may have gotten reimbursed for some
costs, but not all of them. Report all the costs on Form 3903 and
deduct the reimbursements you did receive. The difference will be
a deduction you can use even without having to itemize.

Tip #107:

Doing time. In order to be allowed to use the moving expenses, you must meet the second test, the time test (https://www.irs.gov/publications/p521/ar02.html). Employees and self-employed business owners have to meet different tests about their working period after the move. When you're married, only one spouse must meet one of the tests for the moving deductions to qualify. Let's get the information straight from the IRS.

Time Test for Employees

If you are an employee, you must work full time for at least 39 weeks during the first 12 months after you arrive in the general area of your new job location (39-week test). Full-time employment depends on what is usual for your type of work in your area.

For purposes of this test, the following four rules apply:

- You count only your full-time work as an employee, not any work you do as a self-employed person.
- You do not have to work for the same employer for all 39 weeks.
- You do not have to work 39 weeks in a row.
- You must work full time within the same general commuting area for all 39 weeks.

Time Test for Self-Employed Persons

If you are self-employed, you must work full time for at least 39 weeks during the first 12 months and for a total of at least 78 weeks during the first 24 months after you arrive in the general area of your new job location (78-week test).

For purposes of the time test for self-employed persons, the following three rules apply:

- You count any full-time work you do either as an employee or as a self-employed person.

- You do not have to work for the same employer or be self-employed in the same trade or business for the 78 weeks.

- You must work within the same general commuting area for all 78 weeks.

Incidentally, if you haven't met the time test at the time you file your tax return, don't worry. Go ahead and file as if you had worked for the required number of months. You will only have to amend and take back this deduction if it turns out that you did not keep working long enough. Otherwise, you're just fine.

Read IRS Publication 521 for more information about moving expenses (https://www.irs.gov/publications/p521).

Tip #108:

Business mileage. This is the big deduction for employees and business owners. Be sure to track all your business or job-related miles. These miles count:

- Going from your home to a client's location.

- Going from one client's location to another in the same day.

- Going from your office to a client's location in the same day.

- Going from your main office to a second office.

- Educators going from your school to a second school location in the same day.

- Running business-related errands, like picking up office supplies, going to your PO Box to pick up or drop off your mail, going to the US Post Office to drop off mail, and so on.

- Driving to airports for trips that are primarily work related.

- Driving to conferences, seminars, workshops, and classes.

- Anything else that is specifically work or business related.

The miles that don't count? Commuting miles—driving to/from your home to your business. The nice thing about working from home for yourself or for your employer's benefit is that all mileage starts at your front door.

Tip #109:

Track your mileage carefully using pen/pencil and ink, or any other tools you can find. In Chapter 2, we suggested some tools that can help you with this. Or you can create your own Excel spreadsheet. It doesn't hurt to back up your mileage log with a printout from MapQuest or Google Maps to prove the mileage for each trip. Here is a suggested Excel template heading and MapQuest record. Naturally you can create your own with headings that define your business or job-related travels: http://www.mapquest.com (see image below).

Tip #110:

When you use the mileage method, you may still deduct all the parking lot, parking meter, and toll fees that you must pay when you drive for business. In addition, if you have to pay a separate fee to garage your vehicle (think New York, Chicago, and other places where space is at a premium), you may deduct a portion of that. Use the business percentage of your car use.

	A	B	C	D	E	F	G	H
1		Year		Business or Job Mileage				
2								
3	Date	Starting Point-address	Destination	Business Miles	Business Contact	Business Purpose	If Personal-Enter Miles Here	Map Saved
4								
5	1/15/20XX	1515 Hi Point, Burbank, CA 91501	Huntington Library, 1151 Oxford Rd, San Marino, CA 91108	16.85 miles				Y
6								

For instance, let's say you drive 12,000 miles a year and drove the car for 8,325 miles for business. You may deduct 69.375 percent (8325/12,000) of the garage rental.

Tip #111:

The hidden depreciation in the mileage. Most people don't realize it, but the mileage rate includes a depreciation component. In year-to-year usage, it's not a factor. But when you sell the car, you need to reduce the basis of the car by the amount of depreciation you have deducted on your tax return. So be sure to save your Form 4562 worksheets for all the years you use each vehicle for your job or business. You will need to prepare a spreadsheet showing the number of miles you have claimed each year. In the next column, show the depreciation per mile value. In the final column, show the total depreciation taken that year. Folks who run up the miles during the vehicle's life may find that the depreciation has wiped out their basis altogether. See the example at the end of this Tip.

To read more about how to deduct auto expenses, and using the actual expenses instead of mileage, read chapter 4 of IRS Publication 463, "Transportation" (https://www.irs.gov/publications/p463/ch04.html).

	A	B	C	D	E	F	G
1							
2		Depreciation used in mileage method					
3	YEAR		2012 Cost of Vehicle:		$28,000 Adjustments:		0
4	Vehicle:	Model	Kia	Make	Optima		
5							
6	Year	Dep/cents mile	Total Miles	Business Miles	$ Value of Deprec		
7	Begin Odometer		57				
8	2015	0.24	11353	7625	1830		
9	2014	0.22	13287	8418	1852		
10	2012–2013	0.23	28466	17654	4060		
11	2011	0.22			0		
12	2010	0.23			0		
13	2008–2009	0.21			0		
14	2007	0.19			0		
15	2005–2006	0.17			0		
16	2004–2003	0.16			0		
17	2001–2003	0.15			0		
18							
19					7742		
20							

Tip #112:

There are other ways to make your car pay. Let's explore a few ideas:

- Wrapify and similar advertising companies
- Uber, Lyft, Sidecar, and related quasi-cab services

Tip #113:

Turning your car into a billboard: http://www.wrapify.com/about/.

What a great way to generate income and get a complete makeover for your car. The company wraps your car in advertising. You get paid based on two criteria:

- how much of your car is covered—just panels or the full car
- how many miles you drive

You don't have to pay any fees or invest any money. All you need to qualify is to be over age 21, have a clean driving record, and have a car that is a 2008 model or newer (due to their insurance considerations). Oh yes, one more thing—you need an iPhone or device that runs IOS applications. If you qualify, and they have an advertiser in your area, they will wrap the ad around your car . . . and awaaaaaay you go!

The interesting thing about this revenue is that since it is based on the number of miles you drive, you can suddenly turn your commuting mileage into business mileage. You will report the income on Schedule C and deduct the mileage there as well.

Alas, you are not allowed to drive for Uber et al. when your car is wrapped.

Tip #114:

Uber, Lyft, Sidecar, and related quasi-cab services. The news is full of lawsuits by drivers, cities, and cab unions, as well as conflicts about whether the drivers are employees or independent contractors. For now, the general consensus is that they are independent contractors. That means you are running your own business. You need to do everything a normal business would do with respect to record keeping, cost tracking, mileage tracking, and so on. The good thing is these major companies provide a mileage tracker. Be sure to download the information at least monthly. In fact, it's a good idea to check your data every few days to make sure you get paid for all your passengers. Uber, Lyft, and Sidecar take care of all payments from riders. Sometimes, though, riders will pay you tips. If they pay by credit card, fine. Your company will track that. But if you get paid by cash, it's up to you to track the income. You could, of course, skip reporting the cash. But when the IRS runs audits, they will compare your income to other drivers for the same company. If they typically show that they receive tips and you don't, well . . . you will get a deeper audit.

Many drivers sign up for all the services that operate in their town when they need the hours. Others are only driving part time around their regular jobs, classes, or home-making tasks. Incidentally, this is a terrific job for retirees. It gets you out of the house and talking to people. Who knows, you might even make new friends.

For riders, these are terrific services to call when you know you're going to be drinking. Leave your car at home and get chauffeured to your event or lounge. Then have them come to get you at the end of the evening and take you home. You avoid not only DUIs (tickets and charges for driving under the influence) but also parking tickets for parking in permit-only zones.

(If you've ever had a night out in Hollywood or West Hollywood, you'd know what I mean!)

Tip #115:

Getting a new car. My brother decided to drive for Uber a couple of years ago. His car was a bit too old and worn-out looking. So he bought a new car that he uses primarily for Uber and Lyft driving. It's a good idea to buy a slightly used car and avoid paying for the value that drops the minute you drive off the dealer's lot. Consider buying the dealer's loan car, a salesman's demo car, or the dealers' leased vehicles. Why? It has been serviced by the dealer who is selling it. You can see the full maintenance record. You can get a substantial part of the warranty that's left. Through the dealer, you can buy an extended warranty and keep the dealer's maintenance crew at your beck and call. And if you get a nice dealer like I did when I bought my Infiniti, they will totally clean up and detail your "new" car, replacing soiled carpeting and giving you a car that is just like new. If you don't get your used car from a dealer, please run a CarFax report on the car before buying it or have it inspected by an AAA (American Automobile Association) mechanic: http://www.carfax.com.

With a newly purchased car, you will need to decide if you want to depreciate the car and use actual expenses or use the mileage method. Frankly, with the severe limits on depreciation deductions, you're better off using the mileage method. Think about it—if you drive about 50–100 miles each workday, you'll end up with more than 18,000 miles. Multiply that by 57.5 cents (will be 54 cents in 2016) and you end up with more than $10,000 in mileage deductions. Your actual expenses, even in a car that gets about 23 miles per gallon (mpg), will be about $8,000 or less.

Tip #116:

Get rid of your car. While this isn't a tax tip, it's worth considering. Folks who do everything locally, including a commute within about five miles, should rethink the need for a car. Perhaps a decent bicycle with a basket or two might be a better choice. Let's look at typical car costs:

- Gasoline at approximately $3.50 per gallon based on 23 mpg and 12,000 miles per year = $1,800 (rounded) per year.

- Insurance with enough liability coverage to replace all your assets, uninsured motorist coverage to protect you, and sensible medical and collision coverage = about $1,000 per year.

- Maintenance, tune-ups, lubes, and so on four times a year = $200.

- Biennial smog check = $80 every other year.

- Average licensing for an average vehicle = $125.

- Car washes, monthly, at $15, including tip = $180

- Annual car payments for the first five years at $300 per month = $3,600

- Total = $7,000 per year (rounded)—that's nearly $600 per month!

That doesn't even include parking fees. In contrast, no one charges fees for bikes. Heck, you could get a monthly bus pass to supplement your bike riding, often for $100 or less (https://www.metro.net/riding/fares). And many of the buses even have a place to store bicycles. Not only would it save you a fortune, but it would improve your health, breathing, reduce your weight, and maybe even give you an opportunity to get to know your neighbors a little better.

CHAPTER 9

Deduct Your Medical Expenses and Get Some Money Back

MEDICAL DEDUCTIONS ARE REDUCED by 10 percent of your AGI (or 7.5 percent if you are still under age 65 through December 31, 2016). That makes it pretty hard to generate enough medical expenses to make it worthwhile to even add them up. In fact, as a rule of thumb, for an average household with two jobs earning about $40,000 combined, if unreimbursed medical costs are $4,000 or less, I don't put them through the exercise of gathering the bills. Yet people use medical expense deductions. When and how?

Tip #117:

You can only include in medical expenses those amounts that were actually paid during the taxable year, for which taxpayer received *no* insurance or other reimbursement

during the year. Some common examples of such expenses include:

- Health insurance premiums (or the excess that was not claimed as a self-employed health insurance deduction). Remember to look at your year-end paystub for medical insurance you paid from your paycheck using after-tax dollars.

- Medicare insurance premiums, often deducted from the Social Security checks. Look at the year-end statement from the Social Security Administration for the amount.

- Medical mileage at 23 cents per mile in 2015. (Look up the current mileage rate on the IRS website: http://www.irs .gov/Tax-Professionals/Standard-Mileage-Rates.)

- Tolls and parking fees for medical care or treatments.

- Medical copays—watch out, they add up.

- Prescribed drugs. Even with low copays, they can add up. Especially if you take into account the prescriptions for everyone in the household.

- Medical travel. (We will talk more about that in a few minutes.)

- Costly routine medical and dental treatments that are not reimbursed by insurance, like braces, Lasik surgery, dental implants, and so on.

- Eyeglasses, contacts, and all related solutions and paraphernalia. Our health insurance pays for all this stuff. Yet every time we walk out of LensCrafters, trying to stay within the basic parameters, we each end up paying about $200 out of pocket. I haven't figured this out. Maybe we should be going to Costco? (Did you know that you don't have to be a member to use their optician?)

- Breathing treatments, medicines, apparatus, and portable or stationary air compressors.

- CPAP machines, TENS muscle stimulators, and other torture devices prescribed by physicians.

- Cosmetic surgery for medical purposes—for example, to repair the body and skin after certain operations, fires, accidents, and such, and not purely for personal pleasure.

- Special tutoring, education, or therapy for a child or adult diagnosed with a variety of conditions. (For instance, as a teenager, I had the privilege of getting weekly visual therapy for nearly two years that never actually corrected my condition but was a lot of fun. And I was given weekly speech therapy in both junior high school and high school. This did teach me to speak clearly and to enunciate. Though the sexy voice is all my own.)

- Live-in schools whose purpose is specifically to help treat certain conditions. Military school does not count. This cost is guaranteed to be high enough, so you can use your medical expenses.

- Chiropractic, acupuncture, reiki, and other nonconventional medical treatments if prescribed by your physician. If you pay only $75 per week for treatments, you are looking at nearly $4,000 worth of expenses.

- In-home nursing care. (We'll cover this, too.)

- Nursing home and convalescent home fees. Wow. These can really add up!

Goodness, it does add up, doesn't it? This is just a small list. IRS Publication 502 has a much longer list (https://www.irs.gov/publications/p502). It includes things that might surprise you.

Tip #118:

Deducting costs for a dependent who isn't a dependent.
Sometimes, due to divorce, custody issues, separations or other
sad reasons, your child is filing his or her own tax return and
you are not entitled to claim your child as a dependent. Despite
that, if you pay their medical expenses, you can include medical expenses as deductions on your tax return. You can include
medical expenses you paid for an individual that would have
been your dependent except for the following:

- He or she received gross income of $4,000 or more in 2015
  or $4,050 in 2016.
- He or she filed a joint return for the current year.
- You, or your spouse if filing jointly, could be claimed as a
  dependent on someone else's current year tax return.

What constitutes a dependent for medical deductions if they
are a dependent? Both of the following requirements must be met:

- The person was a qualifying child or a qualifying relative
  (https://www.irs.gov/publications/p502/ar02.html).
- The person was a US citizen or national, or a resident of the
  United States, Canada, or Mexico.

Tip #119:

Speaking of parking fees and tolls. I'll bet you don't have your
parking receipts from your doctor or hospital visits. I certainly
don't. But what I do have is my appointment calendar showing
which doctor, hospital, lab, and so on that I visited on which days.
If you have even one parking receipt from each location (get them
now if you don't have any), then save that. Multiply the usual cost by
the number of visits to each facility. Lay it all out nicely and neatly

on a spreadsheet or document file. Add it all up and put this into your tax folder each year. Fortunately, while I was going to chemo and radiation, my hospital had a special parking area with an attendant (José took good care of us) reserved for cancer patients. The radiology lab validated for parking, but I paid for parking for all the assortment of doctor's visits in most other locations. Even so, I didn't have enough fees to make it worthwhile. But you might.

Tip #120:

In-home nursing care is expensive. Deduct the cost of wages and other amounts paid for nursing services. The services don't need to be performed by a nurse as long as the services are of a kind generally performed by a nurse. This includes caring for the patient's condition, giving medication or changing dressings, as well as bathing and grooming the patient. The services can be provided in your home or another care facility. Generally, only the amount spent for nursing services is a medical expense. If the attendant also provides personal and household services, amounts paid to the attendant must be split between the time spent performing household and personal services and the time spent for nursing services. For instance, someone works for eight hours a day. They spend two hours in the morning bathing your mother, changing bandages, providing medication, making sure she's eating properly, and clearing away the evening's detritus. The next two hours are spent preparing lunch and tidying up the house. The following two hours are spent taking Mom shopping or to visit friends. The last two hours of the day are devoted to cleaning Mom, providing medications, serving dinner, and getting her ready for bed—even if she does stay up reading or watching television after the attendant leaves. Essentially, the care provider devoted half her time to medically relevant activities. So 50 percent of her entire compensation and payroll taxes count as a medical expense.

Tip #121:

Overlooked in-home nursing medical costs. Did you know that the cost of caregiver's meals can be used as medical expenses? Yup. There's more! If you had to pay additional amounts for household upkeep because of the attendant, you can include the extra amounts with your medical expenses. This includes extra rent or utilities you pay because you moved to a larger apartment to provide space for the attendant.

Tip #122:

In-home care means payroll or an agency. If you are paying someone directly, you probably have to put the caregiver(s) on payroll. They are considered household employees if you pay any individual $1,900 or more in 2015 or $2,000 in 2016. You will have to register with the IRS and state as an employer and issue W-2s to all the household workers each year. For the IRS, you report the wages and the taxes withheld on Schedule H, which is included in your tax return (https://www.irs.gov/pub/irs-pdf/f1040sh.pdf). However, your state may require regular quarterly payroll tax returns and deposits. The truth is payroll reporting is as detailed, complicated, and time consuming for one employee as it is for 25–50 employees. If just reading this makes you want to tear your hair out, turn this task over to a payroll service or your tax professional. True, it will cost you about $75–$125 per quarter, but it's worth it to take the pressure off. (Search for "nanny tax.")

The other option is to hire the attendant through an agency. The agency will put them on their payroll and take care of all the taxes, reports, and so on. Make sure they have a payroll. If not, use a different agency. But using an agency typically means paying at least 25 to 30 percent for their costs and profits. Suppose this person will cost you an extra $25 per day. That could mean as much as $700 extra per month (25 × 365 divided by 12) when your mom or child needs daily care. Frankly, paying $125 per quarter for a payroll service is much cheaper than paying $2,100 extra per quarter to an agency.

Oh yes, if you are using the Schedule H route, remember to increase your federal withholding at work, or raise your quarterly estimated tax payments to cover the additional Social Security, Medicare, and Unemployment taxes that will be due with your ultimate tax return.

Tip #123:

The "Home!" Yup, sometimes you just have no choice. You have to send your loved one to a nursing or convalescent home or facility. It could be due to extreme age, dementia, or to get rehabilitation after an accident or physical event. In this case, practically all the costs are deductible as medical expenses.

Unless! My mother is in her nineties. She called us all a few years back and asked to be moved to the "home." We thought her residence expenses would be fully deductible—until I read this: "If an individual is able to perform at least two activities of daily living, the rental costs are not deductible. Activities of daily living are eating, toileting, transferring, bathing, dressing, medication management and continence" (https://www.irs.gov/publications/p502/ar02.html#en_US_2014_publink1000178974).

Uh, Mother can do all those things herself. There goes a whopping deduction! Oh well.

On the other hand, if someone is unable to perform at least two activities of daily living without substantial assistance from another individual, or requires substantial supervision to be protected from severe cognitive impairment (a.k.a. Alzheimer's), then qualified long-term care services will be necessary and deductible.

Even if your loved ones can take care of themselves, if they are getting medical or nursing care, those costs are deductible. In my mother's case, the campus has all kinds of doctors.

She is constantly being poked and prodded and tested, right on the premises, for a variety of age and pain-related issues. If your loved ones are in a similar situation, you might want to try to get paperwork to define what part of their rent is for the medical care. Whose medical expenses may you deduct? Yours, your spouse's, and your dependents'. This includes the cost of meals and lodging in the home if a principal reason for being there is to get medical care.

Tip #124:

Medical travel. Let's look at the basics. Medical travel includes the costs for the patient and a (one) companion/caregiver—up to $50 per night each (no deduction for meals). Medical travel for treatment outside of the country is deductible. Remember to pick up the cost of medical miles if you're driving and the cost of airfare, shuttles, cabs, and so on if you are not driving.

Tip #125:

Medical travel bonus. Did you know that medical travel outside the country is deductible? Yes it is. That means the airfare to some exotic locale with lodging limited to $50 per night each for the patient and companion. The treatment may require the patient to stay in that country for several weeks until the full set of procedures are complete. The lodging for all those days is allowable if it is impractical to travel back and forth for the treatment. For instance, sometimes you need to get a series of operations or procedures (like dental implants, medical lap-banding, medical cosmetic surgery, or burn treatments). After each procedure, it's necessary to wait a few days before the next step can be taken safely. In some cases, the treatment, travel, and living expenses are still cheaper than it would cost here in the United States. Speaking of dental work, my friend and I priced the cost of her dental needs here and in India. The costs were so much lower in India. Even after adding in the cost of the airfare, lodging, and meals while waiting for the entire series of operations to be completed, the overall cost was still lower than the US cost at a local dental surgeon's and facility. The bonus? She got to visit with her family and friends for a month while deducting the whole trip as a medical expense. Naturally, if the main purpose of the trip is a vacation without any real medical validity . . . no deduction. So before hitting the international medical circuit, get a valid prescription or course of treatment, in writing, from a legitimate, licensed US medical practitioner.

Incidentally, some medical facilities around the world are aware of this tax trick. They will make it easy for you to comply with US laws. Since their costs are so much lower, the foreign medical facilities attract patients by providing a full-service facility—medical services, lodging, and meals all rolled into the price. After all, patients need to remain under medical supervision until the physicians are sure everything is properly completed. Do your research. You may be surprised at the high level of competence you find. But beware—there are also charlatans who can do you great harm.

Tip #126:

Not quite a dependent, but almost? These days, we often find ourselves in that sandwich generation—squeezed between helping to support our children and our parents, who are living longer than ever before. In order to claim someone as a dependent, we need to be paying more than half their support. But costs are so high that it might require several people to chip in to cover all the costs to support a particular person. Believe it or not, the IRS has a solution for you. It's Form 2120, the Multiple Support Declaration (https://www.irs.gov/pub/irs-pdf/f2120.pdf). Enter the name and Social Security number of the person being supported. This person will not claim his or her own exemption on the personal tax return. Then get each person to sign this form every year that you are all jointly supporting someone. Allocate the deduction to you first, since you came up with the idea. Next year, and thereafter, take turns giving the dependency exemption to each person participating in the support.

Tip #127:

When medical expenses are high, reduce regular IRA account and retirement plan balances. When someone dies, the heirs have to pay taxes on all the money in regular IRA accounts and most retirement accounts. Money held in Roth IRA accounts is not taxed to heirs or to the living (after the account has been funded for five years). Suppose you had a way to pull the money out of an IRA or retirement account while you (or your loved one) are alive without paying much, if anything, in taxes. Would you do it? You bet!

Well, one CPA didn't think to do this for his client. Many years ago, I met the nicest man who was being audited for his high medical expenses. It turned out that his CPA wasn't paying attention to two issues. The first was that he didn't tell Wally that the round-the-clock caregivers for his mother, and his own caregiver, all needed to be on payroll. Wally didn't want to get them into trouble by fixing that for the audit, so he gracefully allowed the IRS to disallow all his expenses. And the second oversight was that Wally had more than half a million dollars in his 401(k) account. The CPA could have been advising Wally to move that money to a Roth IRA for five years or more. By paying his help legitimately, Wally could have rolled over at least $30,000 a year, tax-free. I had Wally start doing it immediately. But he died two years later, leaving more than $400,000 still in the fully taxable retirement account.

Here's how you can do this for yourself and your heirs:

- Compute the right amount to draw out of the retirement accounts so the income from the draws will be balanced by deductible medical expenses.

- Draw out the funds if the person doesn't need the cash in order to pay the medical expenses. Add the amounts to income. Roll the funds to a Roth IRA. Voila! You have converted the taxable accounts to tax-free accounts.

- Rinse, lather, repeat. Do this each year until all the IRAs and retirement accounts are rolled over to Roths or used up to pay medical expenses.

Tip #128:

This tip provides no tax deduction, but here's how you can avoid gift and estate taxes when paying someone else's medical expenses. You may pay anyone's medical expenses as a gift without any gift tax limitations providing you make the payments directly to the medical provider. Normally, gifts are limited to $14,000 per person, per year (2014–2016) before the giver must face gift taxes. In this case, if you have a friend or family member who needs your help, pay the doctor, hospital, lab, or other medical provider directly. You won't need to file a gift tax return for these gifts, no matter how much you spend. Since this person isn't your dependent, you won't get a medical expense deduction, though. One warning: if the person for whom you are paying changes his or her mind and backs out of the medical services, gets a refund, or gets insurance reimbursements, they must pay you back. If they don't, even if you don't know about it, you might be faced with surprise gift taxes. So know your patient well, or never contribute more than $14,000 toward any person's medical care in any one year.

Tip #129:

You need money to help pay your medical bills. Crowdfunding sites like GoFundMe, YouCaring, GiveForward, and others have cropped up all over the Internet. Generally, when you use sites like this, the funds you receive tend to be considered income by the IRS. How can you avoid causing a tax problem when you help someone? Easy, set up the campaign properly. Here are four easy steps to keep you, and the friend in need, out of tax trouble:

1. When raising money for someone's medical expenses, set up the crowdfunding account and bank account in the name and SSN of the recipient—not yours!

2. Do *not* offer anything in return—no ebooks, no t-shirts, no nothing! Doing that allows the IRS to think you've turned this appeal into a sales opportunity.

3. Do *not* promise the donors a tax deduction. Since you are not a registered nonprofit (exempt) organization, none of the contributions are deductible donations. They are all gifts.

4. Use all the money to pay for things you said you needed to pay. Don't get into the habit of defrauding the people who were kind enough to help you. Sometimes you raise more money than you requested. If there is any money left over, don't worry. It's yours. If you are ill enough and/or broke enough to turn to crowdfunding, you probably need the extra money for living expenses or follow-up treatments. These funds are still not taxable, since all the contributions were voluntary gifts. Of course, you can opt to donate those excess funds to charity or to someone else's crowdfunding campaign. Spread the help and the love.

Tip #130:

If your medical expenses were paid by others or via crowd-funding, do you get to deduct the medical expenses if you didn't pay them yourself? As it turns out, you may. There is a very clear and specific Tax Court Memo from 2010 that addresses this issue. Should you ever find yourself in this situation and get audited, use this citation to settle your audit. Consider reading it. It's quite interesting (TC Memo 2010-286, *Lang v. Commissioner*: http://www.ustaxcourt.gov/InOpHistoric/La5ng .TCM.WPD.pdf).

Tip #131:

You don't need no stinkin' medical deduction. There are ways to handle medical expenses without using any deductions at all. The best way to do that is by paying for medical expenses with untaxed income. These are two options, often overlooked, because they are misunderstood:

- Flexible Spending Accounts (FSAs)
- Health Saving Accounts or Arrangements (HSAs)

FSAs are provided by your employer. HSAs can be set up by your employer, or you can set one up for yourself.

Tip #132:

Flexible Spending Accounts (FSAs). This used to be worth $5,000 right off the top of your wages without any taxes at all being taken out. Starting in 2012, Congress dropped this amount. Today, the limit is $2,550. There's still a tax saving here, but it is literally half the value. So what does all this mean? When you know that your out-of-pocket medical expenses during the year will average $50 per month or more, it's worth signing up for the FSA. Please be realistic about your medical expense projection. You run the risk of losing your money if you overestimate your expenses. Assuming you figured correctly, it's a great deal, since you're spending the money anyway. How do you set it up? During open enrollment, or whenever your company schedule permits, tell your payroll department to deduct up to $2,550 (you decide how much) from your paycheck over the 12-month period. As you pay for eligible medical expenses for yourself, family members, or dependents (or almost dependents, see Tip #118), just send in the receipts to the administrator and get your money back. Meanwhile, for tax purposes, your W-2 will show a lower income amount in all the boxes—wages, Social Security Income, and Medicare Income. Since you're going to be spending money on these medical expenses anyway, why not skip the taxes altogether?

What happens if you don't run up enough expenses to get your money back by the end of the year? It's important to understand this issue. Find out if your employer participates in the two-and-a-half-month extension, allowing you to get medical services and pay medical bills until March 15 of the following year. If they do, you will have two and a half extra months to get your money back. If your employer doesn't offer that option, review your medical expenditures by October of each year. See how much money you have not yet gotten back. Are there receipts you have not submitted yet, like prescriptions, contact lenses, or routine medical supplies? If yes, submit them immediately. If not, it's time to get new eyeglasses or contact lenses, or visit the dentist or . . . what do you still need to do? One year, I used up the money by getting those customized shoe inserts, orthotics. It seemed expensive to me, but I had overestimated our medical expenses and this was the only way to get something for our money. As it turns out, in the right pair of shoes, those orthotics are actually quite comfortable. Read more about

FSAs in IRS Publication 969 (https://www.irs.gov/publications/p969/ar02.html).

Tip #133:

Health Saving Accounts or Arrangements (HSAs). These are quite a bit more complicated, but they also allow you to stow away a lot more money. Individuals may contribute up to $3,350, and families up to $6,750 (https://www.irs.gov/pub/irs-drop/rp-15-30.pdf) for 2016. Visit the IRS website for update information, since this amount changes each year due to inflation. The money may be funded by an individual or an employer. Once the money is in the HSA (set up as part of the Health Savings Arrangement), if you don't touch the money, you can leave it there to grow until you get old or face an emergency. Kind of like a second IRA. The contributions to this account can come off the top of your wages if you have a job. Or your employer can pay the money for you without you facing any taxes. If you are self-employed, it will be an adjustment to income. (So the contribution won't reduce your self-employment taxes.)

On the other hand, the HSA is designed to cover your out-of-pocket medical expenses when you have a high-deductible insurance plan. So you are definitely allowed to use the account to pay for your medical expenses. In fact, the insurance provider can give you a debit card to use in pharmacies, hospitals, and other medical establishments. For 2016, a high deductible health plan means the plan has a deductible of at least $1,300 for individuals and $2,600 for families.

Tip #134:

HSA reporting. The one drawback to this is that the HSA administrator will send you a Form 5498-SA at the end of the year showing how much money you spent from the account (https://

www.irs.gov/pub/irs-pdf/f1099sa.pdf). In order to avoid pay-ing taxes and penalties on these expenditures, you must attach a Form 8889 to your tax return (https://www.irs.gov/pub/irs -access/f8889_accessible.pdf). Yes, this *is* a pain. And ever since this form was created, taxpayer and tax professionals alike have struggled to get it to work so that all the penalties are cleared. Definitely see a tax pro if you used your HSA to pay for medical expenses. One more important thing to know about these debit cards: you can use them for anything at all in a pharmacy or cer-tain other places. In other words, you can buy food, beverages, greeting cards, make-up, and so on. The IRS is wise to this. Just showing that the charge took place in a pharmacy, CVS, Wal-greens, and so on is not enough. You must have the receipt for the purchase, and it must be for a legitimate medical expense. If not, you will be paying taxes and penalties on the noneligible purchase. Be sure to look at the receipt or invoice carefully. For instance, one client had payments for doctor-prescribed mas-sages. Her masseuse changed the name of her business from "her name, Licensed Massage Practitioner" to something with the word "Euphoria" in it. Boy was that a red flag among the medical receipts. If you face something like that, get a better receipt and/or copy of the doctor's prescription sending you to this therapist. The client got audited. After the folks at the IRS had a good laugh, they approved all the expenses.

Note: Not all states recognize the HSA, so find out if this works with your state tax laws. Otherwise, your contributions will be taxable on the state level.

HSAs really are more complicated than they should be. There is a lot more to this tax break than I have summarized here. In fact, there are a couple more medical-type tax breaks. Please read more about them in IRS Publication 969 (https://www.irs .gov/publications/p969).

Tip #135:

Caregivers, get your money back! Over the years, several of my clients and readers have received income from the government to care for their own family members. Sometimes they provide the care in the caregiver's home; other times they go to their family member's home. (I must admit that I always wondered how they even learned about the programs. I think social workers let them know about these opportunities. They are offered through Medicaid. You should be able to find information about these opportunities in your state by searching the Internet.)

OK, let's focus on the income. For years we reported those payments as taxable income. Then came a time when we tax professionals were getting conflicting information about whether the income was taxable or not. On January 3, 2014, the IRS finally settled the argument. They issued a notice telling us that this income is specifically not taxable (https://www.irs.gov/Individuals/Certain-Medicaid-Waiver-Payments-May-Be-Excludable-From-Income). Yippee! The IRS said they "will treat these Medicaid waiver payments as difficulty of care payments excludable from gross income under § 131 of the Internal Revenue Code."

What does this mean to you? It means that you don't have to report this income any longer. Better yet, if you reported this income in the past, you might be able to file an amended return (Form 1040X) to get a refund for the taxes you paid on this income. You can amend a tax return to get a refund within three years of the filing date of the tax return. Or, if you paid the taxes later because you were short of funds, you may get a refund within two years after you paid the taxes if that turns out to be later.

For instance, you finally finished paying $2,000 of your 2011 IRS balance due on September 12, 2014. You can recover this payment until September 11, 2016. Normally, if you filed the 2011 tax return on October 15, 2012, you could only get a refund until October 14, 2015. Sometimes there is an advantage to filing late.

CHAPTER 10

Charity Deductions Begin at Home

Americans are really generous people. Whenever there is a flood, earthquake, fires, disaster, or refugee situation anywhere in the world, Americans step up and chip in with money, time, and resources. We do this as individuals, through nonprofit organizations, and via our tax dollars as well. My husband pointed out that we don't seem to get the same degree of generosity from individuals or governments when the United States faces similar needs. But that won't stop us. We are Super-Kind!

Some of our donations generate charitable contribution deductions. Some don't. And some are outright thefts by charlatans. Let's sort through the noise and help you find the truth so you can continue to be generous and not embittered by thieves.

Tip #136:

Every time there is a major disaster or event, charities spring up to help out. That's good, right? Well . . . not so good. Many of them are fakes designed to tap into the outpouring of love and money. Confine your contributions to established charities. If you've never heard of it, it probably isn't real. There are two ways to find out if a charity is legitimate via the IRS:

- Look them up on the IRS list of exempt organizations. This list will tell if you the charity exists, if they have been suspended or are active, how much of your deduction you can use this year, and if the charity has filed the Form 990-N postcard (for very small charities): https://www.irs .gov/Charities-&-Non-Profits/Exempt-Organizations-Select -Check. This resource will let you see the data entered on the Form 990-N, if they were small enough to file one.

- Call the IRS at 1-877-829-5500 if you think the charity is too new to be on the list.

Tip #137:

Learn how organizations use your money. Most exempt organizations (except "churches," which include all religious denominations) must file a version of Form 990 every single year. This is public information. You can go online and see their report. This can help you decide if they are using enough of your funds for the intended purpose—or using too much for the administrators' compensation, trips, and personal benefit. Or just wasting it. Here are some places you can find that information:

- GuideStar is one of the most established resources online and the one at the top of the search engines. They provide

summary information about the organization's total reve-
nues and expenses. To see the tax returns, you need to set
up a free account and log in. For more detailed information,
like tax reports going back more than three years and information about officers and more, you must pay for access—
http://www.guidestar.org/Home.aspx.

- The Foundation Center allows you to look up your organization and gives you instant access to their tax forms for
  free without any log-ins. So you can look up your charity
  anonymously—http://foundationcenter.org/findfunders/
  990finder.

  ○ To help you understand what the tax return means, let's
    look up a charity I know well, since many members of
    my family have been active in it for over half a century,
    Shelters for Israel (http://www.sheltersforisrael.com/
    about-us). It's a very small organization started by Ho-
    locaust survivors pooling their winnings at their weekly
    card game. Their mission is to provide housing, day care
    centers, playgrounds, and other facilities for children,
    students, disadvantaged youth, and immigrants. You can
    see the list of the projects they have funded since 1950
    (http://www.sheltersforisrael.com/list-of-all-projects).
    They claim that all their funds go toward their projects.
    Let's see what we can learn about them and if their claims
    are true, OK?

  ○ First, we look at the overview of their Form 990 filings for
    the last three years. We learn they are in compliance and
    have been filing. Here is the summary:

ORGANIZATION NAME	STATE	YEAR	FORM	PAGES	TOTAL ASSETS	EIN
Shelters for Israel	CA	2013	990	20	$209,588.00	95-6118813
Shelters for Israel	CA	2012	990EZ	15	$156,519.00	95-6118813
Shelters for Israel	CA	2011	990EZ	13	$382,326.00	95-6118813

Clicking on the link (under the name) to see the tax return (http://990s.foundationcenter.org/990_pdf_archive/956/956118813/956118813_201312_990.pdf?_ga=1.2521678 87.7586187.1446561556), we learn:

- They spent more than they raised in 2013 (page 1 of Form 990).
- They pay absolutely no salaries to any of the officers (page 7 of Form 990) or anyone else (page 10 of Form 990).
- They charge no membership dues. Their fundraising events (an annual banquet and advertising/tributes in their monthly newsletter) raised nearly $226,000, while they spent less than $8,000 on food and related costs (page 9 of Form 990). That's an astonishing 96.5 percent net return on the event.
- They spend minute sums on accounting and rent "occupancy"—totaling less than $500 (page 10 of Form 990).
- Their highest expenditures, besides the costs of putting on events and funding their projects, are printing and postage, about $18,500, which is less than 8.5 percent of the funds they raised (page 10 of Form 990).
- Most importantly, 91.4 percent of the funds they raise are used for the charitable purpose intended. However, since they did spend more on projects ($230,500) than they raised ($217,869) in 2013, they actually spent more than 107 percent on programs. Compare that to the Los Angeles County Fair Association, which has been paying its chief executive about $900,000 a year while showing losses of millions of dollars every year (http://www.latimes.com/local/california/la-me-fairplex-bonuses-20151103-story.html).

- GrantSpace.org maintains a page where you can find a list of sources providing information about exempt organizations: http://grantspace.org/tools/knowledge-base/Funding -Research/Forms-990-and-990-PF/finding-990-990-pfs.

Tip #138:

Deducting money. You would think it would be pretty straightforward to claim a deduction for donations of money to legitimate exempt or religious organizations, right? Well, not quite that easy. I cannot emphasize how important it is to get proper receipts from the organization for each and every donation of $250 or more. What is proper? The receipt must show the following:

- The date of the donation.
- The legal name of the organization.
- Its mailing address. (It also helps to have a phone number.)
- The taxpayer ID number (TIN)—*very* important.
- The amount of the donation.
- A statement that says you did not receive any products or services for your donation, or a statement that spells out the value of products of services you received. (For instance, suppose you pay $250 per person for a fund-raising banquet. The receipt should show that you received an amount, say, $50 worth of food and goody-bag stuff.)

Not having all this information for every single donation means you can lose the deduction if you're audited.

Tip #139:

Get receipts on time. You absolutely must have the receipt in your hot little hands before you file your tax return, or before the legal deadline to file your tax return (if you are filing late). The receipt must be dated before you file your tax return. This is imperative. When you are audited, even if you can prove that you paid $10,000 to your favorite charity—with all the cancelled checks and a letter from the charity dated during the audit, a personal note from the Pope, Chief Rabbi, or Imam—you will lose the deduction. The IRS auditor has no authority to approve it. IRS Appeals cannot grant you the deduction. Even the Tax Court cannot give you the deduction, though they will be sympathetic. Why is there no leeway? Internal Revenue Code Section 170 (Sec 170(f)(8)(C)) has this totally rigid provision:

(C) Contemporaneous

For purposes of subparagraph (A), an acknowledgment shall be considered to be contemporaneous if the taxpayer obtains the acknowledgment on or before the earlier of—

(i) the date on which the taxpayer files a return for the taxable year in which the contribution was made, or (ii) the due date (including extensions) for filing such return.

There have been many court cases where people did have proof that they made donations worth many thousands of dollars. But the verifications from the exempt organizations were dated long after the acceptable date. As a result, when my clients tithe or make major contributions, I ask to see the receipts before we file the tax return. In fact, last year, one client had to struggle to get a receipt for a $10,000 contribution because the organization was run by volunteers with no official administrator.

To avoid the problem of gathering receipts for your many donations of $250 or more, consider contributing to a donor-advised fund. Read TaxMama's December 2015 article in her MarketWatch.com Tax Watch column: http://www.marketwatch

.com/story/how-to-get-a-big-tax-write-off-while-doing-a-good
-deed-2015-12-17.

Tip #140:

No deduction for disguised donations. Yes, yes, the IRS knows
that the $2,000 per month tuition to your child's religious school
isn't really a donation to the synagogue. It really is tuition—and
is not a deductible contribution. What part of the tuition to religious schools may you deduct, if any? Naturally, none of the
tuition itself. But what if they call part of it a donation, say $300
per month? If this is a mandatory payment for every student, it's
not a donation. Donations are voluntary. It's just another way
to disguise tuition. Sometimes the invoices have a line where
you can add an amount as a donation. *That* would be deductible. Make sure the school totals that separately and provides a
separate receipt monthly or a summary of the donations at the
end of the year. The IRS audits religious schools all the time and
"teaches" the administrators about how to separate tuition
and donations—after making a list of parents to audit.

Tip #141:

Cash in the collection plate. Listening to an inspiring sermon,
how can you help but contribute generously when the plate
comes around? Please, don't restrain your enthusiasm. Instead,
carry your checkbook and contribute on paper. This way, the organization has your information. They can create a report at the
end of the year showing how much you contributed. Without that
written receipt, you won't be able to deduct anything over $250.

Tip #142:

Cash to street people. There are over half a million people who
really are homeless (https://www.hudexchange.info/resources/

documents/2014-AHAR-Part1.pdf), living on the street or in temporary shelters, begging for handouts. It's impossible not to feel sympathy, especially with the shaky economy, knowing that this could be you. There are two reasons to think twice about giving them cash:

- You don't get a deduction for donating to a person—only to a registered exempt organization or religious organization.

- Sadly, there are so many phonies out there who do this for a living because it's free money. It's hard to tell if someone really is hard up. So if you do help them, just do it out of love and faith and pray that they pass on the goodness to others in need. But no deduction.

  ○ I saw one guy at the freeway off-ramp daily for about a year. People gave him cash. I estimated that he probably collected at least $100 a day, at least five days a week. In only fifty weeks, he was collecting about $25,000–$50,000 without paying any taxes. Are you making that much money?

  ○ Another woman stood in the post office parking lot for about two years with a sign saying that she had cancer and needed help. Well, being in the middle of that experience myself, I was aware of several programs designed to help her. I offered her information on where to get funding, care, free wigs, courses, transportation, and all. She pushed me away and told me to mind my own business—and went after another postal patron to get cash. (We later learned she was, in fact, a liar.)

Tip #143:

Cash for silent auctions, regular charity auctions, bazaars, and so on. It's fun to go to the special events where people donate things to help an organization raise money. You may not deduct the value of your purchase. So if you bid on something and get it at a bargain, there is no deduction at all. If you pay more than the retail value, be sure to get a receipt that shows that the excess amount is a contribution.

Tip #144:

Donating time. Ah, this is the most precious, irreplaceable resource there is. How does Congress value your time? (You do know that they write the laws, not the IRS, right?) As far as Congress is concerned, your time is worthless. So whether you are donating your professional services or just your personal sweat, there is no deduction at all for time. Period. Don't argue with the IRS. It's been tried, and people have failed.

Tip #145:

Donating money to specific people. The Tax Code (IRC Sec 170 (c)(2)(C)) has a prohibition against making a donation to benefit a specific person. People try to make a sizeable donation to a college, for instance, so they will accept a particular student or provide that specific student with a scholarship. Not deductible. The donation may not have strings on it. Or someone in your community is about to lose her home and the pastor asks everyone to chip in and help her. Even if the donations go to the church, there is no deduction because it's specifically earmarked for an individual. To raise funds for people without any tax effect on the person receiving the money, read Tip #129. Regardless, there is no charitable contribution deduction.

Tip #146:

Donating things, starting with minor amounts. We all do the year-end thing where we clean out our closets and attics and take all the clean (hopefully) and usable clothing, small appliances, games, and knickknacks to our favorite charity or thrift shop. Make sure you get a receipt for your donations each time that you drop off your bags and/or boxes. You can get away with claiming a deduction of up to $500 without too much substantiation, aside from the receipts. Figure that each bag is worth about $25–$30 and each box is worth $50–$100, depending on what's in it.

Tip #147:

Donating things and getting a higher deduction for the minor stuff. When I ask my clients to make a list of all the things that went into the bags and boxes, an amazing thing happens. Those three bags and two boxes that were originally worth about $275 now prove to be worth well over $1,000. How did that happen? Instead of bunching together some amorphous junk, you now have a detailed list of each item of clothing, each appliance, each toy or piece of furniture, some of which might have originally been quite pricey. It's a good idea to take pictures of all the things you're donating, especially if they are pretty, clean, and make your donation look good. This will help support your list of goodies. One of the best free tools you can use to establish the current market value for each item is Intuit's ItsDeductible software (https://turbotax.intuit.com/personal-taxes/itsdeductible). The software has the values built in. True, it can take you an hour or two to enter each item one by one. But once you're done, you might be able to demonstrate that your so-so $275 bags and boxes really contain items that add up to $1,475. Do this before completing your tax return so you can put the printout and pictures into your tax file for the year. An extra $1,200 of deductions could net you anywhere from $180 to over $300 in federal and state tax savings. That's not too bad for an hour or two of work, is it?

Tip #148:

Donating expensive things. When you have something very special to donate, like a work of art, the rights to a piece of music, especially something worth $5,000 or more, you need to use a special tax form, Form 8283 (https://www.irs.gov/pub/irs-pdf/f8283.pdf). You must also get a formal, written appraisal, and the professional appraiser must sign Part III on page 2 of the Form 8283. In cases like this, I ask the appraiser to sign at least three copies of the form. One for the IRS, one in case the state wants an original, and a third copy for the taxpayer's own files.

- Sometimes you can get an objective valuation for some things from the retail or wholesale seller. But only do this if the item's value is under $5,000—and get the value in writing on their forms.

- We needed objective valuations on my father-in-law's two electric wheelchairs. The vendor who sold them to him told us his trade organization had advised all sellers to stop providing written appraisals. Uh oh. Where do we get a value?

- It turns out that in California there is a special designation called a Probate Referee (http://www.sco.ca.gov/eo_probate_contact.html). These folks are empowered to provide valuations for items in estates for the Probate Court. Using the local referee, who came to us, we were able to get the official reports, valuations, and signatures for a fraction of what some other appraiser might have charged. She was delightful to work with and helpful with some other contacts we needed. See if there is anything like this in your state.

- *Note: The IRS doesn't always accept appraisals at face value. If you don't get a professional appraisal done properly, it's quite likely that the IRS will audit and dispute your valuation* (https://www.irs.gov/publications/p561/ar02.html).

*Using someone flaky who overstates the value of your do-
nation could get you penalties of 20–40 percent of your tax
underpayments* (https://www.irs.gov/publications/p561/ar02
.html#d0e1964).

For more information on the IRS's perspective about putting
a value on your donations, read IRS Publication 561, "Determining the Value of Donated Property" (https://www.irs.gov/
publications/p561).

Tip #149:

Appraisal fees. When you pay a professional for the valuation
of donated property, the fee is not a charitable contribution.
However, you may claim the deduction further down on the
Schedule A as a miscellaneous itemized deduction, reduced by
2 percent of AGI (https://www.irs.gov/publications/p526/ar02
.html#en_US_2014_publink1000229700).

Tip #150:

Donating vehicles. The best tip that I can give you here is—
don't. Period. It's just way too much trouble. First of all, if the
vehicle really is in good condition, why are you donating it? Why
aren't you using it as a trade-in or selling it? If you do donate
it, you have to jump through so many hoops and get specific
paperwork with the valuation of the vehicle. You need a Form
1098-C from the organization to which you donated the vehicle
(https://www.irs.gov/pub/irs-pdf/f1098c.pdf). You might not
get the paperwork from them until after the organization sells
it, which might not happen before you file your tax return—
which means you don't really know the value of your donation.
Taxpayers have found this process incredibly frustrating and
often take it out on the tax professional. Folks, we don't write

the laws. We just try to help you handle them correctly. So, I repeat, don't donate vehicles. Sell them and give the money to charity if you like, but avoid vehicle donations like the plague. P.S.—if you donate your vehicle to one of those places that also gives you money or trips to Las Vegas or some such thing (that you might never use), you still have to reduce your donation by the face value of the money or goodies you received.

Tip #151:

You love to make donations but get no tax benefit from them. I stumbled across this problem because one of my favorite clients tithes—or more than tithes, actually. She donates more than $10,000 per year to her church. But since her income is mostly retirement, Social Security, and paper losses from her rental properties, she doesn't need to itemize her deductions. The donation is wasted on her as far as tax benefits are concerned. Do we want her to stop making the donations and supporting her church? Of course not. What's the solution? She can gift the money to her son and daughter-in-law. They make the donation to the church, now that it's their money. They get to claim the $10,000 deduction. See what a clean, elegant solution that is? Everyone wins.

Tip #152:

Tax deductions are limited. Depending on what you contribute to what kind of charity, your charitable contribution deductions are limited to 20 percent, 30 percent, or 50 percent of your AGI. I will not bore you with the details. This only matters when you donate appreciated assets (things that are worth more now than when you bought them), donate to foundations, or a couple of other special situations. If you are lucky enough to be in that position, you should be working with a tax professional to plan your giving. But do read what the IRS has to say about these limits (https://www.irs.gov/publications/p526/ar02.html) in Publication 526 (https://www.irs.gov/publications/p526).

Tip #153:

Speaking of limits, what do you do with the deductions you cannot use this year? Good question. You can take those deductions next year, or the year after that, and so on, for up to 15 years. Read about carryovers (https://www.irs.gov/publications/p526/ar02.html). That's why it was important to have my client stop tithing to her church. She already has enough contribution carryovers that it will take her a few years to use them up. We wouldn't want to waste them, would we?

Tip #154:

Why would you want to make a $100,000 nondeductible donation? For several years, we have had a special provision in the Internal Revenue Code allowing senior citizens to make donations directly from their IRA accounts to the charity or charities of their choice (https://www.irs.gov/Retirement-Plans/Charitable-Donations-from-IRAs). This was targeted at folks ages 70½ or above who faced taking required minimum deposits (RMDs) from their retirement accounts—or face hefty penalties. This option requires that the withdrawal is transferred directly to the charity (called a Qualified Direct Transfer, or QDT). We'll talk a lot more about this in the chapter on seniors and retirement.

Note: This has been made a permanent part of the Internal Revenue Code as Section 112 of the PATH Act of 2015. Please see Bonus Tip #270 for more details.

Tip #155:

**Services are not deductible, but volunteering can be profit-
able.** Volunteering often comes with costs. As you know, we may
deduct our volunteer mileage (a whopping 14 cents per mile),
but there are other costs as well. To participate in certain events,
we might have to buy and wear uniforms. Those costs, as well
as laundering costs, are deductible. We bring food or goodies
to supply other volunteers. We print things to hand out, often
at our own expense. We might need supplies, tools, and other
things that we only use in association with our volunteer activities. We might take our charges out (children, homeless people,
seniors, etc.) to lunch or dinner as part of our volunteer function.
For camping with Scouts, we might need camping supplies that
are only used for these events. How can you deduct these costs?
Back to TaxMama's mantra: *document, document, document!*
Keep excellent records (appointment books, logs, and such), receipts, and detailed notes about the odd or unusual expenses. If
you can, submit an overall report to the charity or organization
with a list of the costs. Have them write you a "Thank you" letter
showing the amount of your out-of-pocket contributions. This
will provide additional substantiation for the legitimacy of the
costs, as they relate to the charity's activities. One of my broad-
caster friends and his wife are actively involved in several charities raising money to research his wife's illness, their synagogue,
and other organizations. One year, they spent about $30,000,
split between money and volunteering costs. Their CPA did not
explain the record-keeping requirements to them. They ended
up with a massive IRS audit. After spending several hours with
them, I was able to help them save about half their deductions.
But without proper and timely receipts, they lost well over
$10,000 of deductions and faced more than six months of audit
hell. Do you want to do a better job? See how the "Crazy Cat
Lady" handled her records and won the right to her deductions

in Tax Court in the case of *Van Dusen v. Commissioner* (http://taxmama.com/tax-quips/crazy-cat-lady-takes-on-irs).

Tip #156:

Volunteering doesn't have to be about depressing charities. It can be fun, too! You can even get intangible rewards. Who knows, you may even meet celebrities. Helping out at a road rally raising money for the homeless, I got to meet and chat with baby boomer idols Connie Stevens, Stella Stevens, Zsa Zsa Gabor, Billy Barty, Chad Everett, and Dorian and Nancy Harewood with their new baby, along with several other delightful celebrities. Speaking of silent auctions, since the event appeared to be in danger of raising too little money, Connie Stevens bid outrageously high amounts for a variety of objects, simply to ensure the event reached its financial goal. Ms. Stevens is definitely one class act.

Tip #157:

Here are some fun ideas for volunteering. They are not only fun, they are good exercise, you get to meet interesting people and, who knows, you might even end up meeting the love of your life—your intended!

- My long-ago dental hygienist, Linda Baker, author of *Cake Girl* (http://www.amazon.com/Cake-Girl-Reasonably-Sweetest-Frosting/dp/1503138119), used to be a tour guide and docent for the Los Angeles Conservancy (https://www.laconservancy.org). That brought her into contact with tourist, locals, politicians, and even celebrities.

- Virginia Lawrence always loved ships. As a widow, she got involved with the Official Los Angeles Tall Ships (http://www.tallshipsfestivalla.com) and is having the time of her life helping schoolchildren learn the ropes (pun intended). She goes on cruises, climbs riggings, and gets younger, more vital, and healthier every day.

- Our California Society of Enrolled Agents (CSEA) members used to march in the annual Pasadena Doo Dah Parade (http://pasadenadoodahparade.info/about). We would wear our green "We SpEAk Tax" long-sleeved T-shirts (it's cold in California in November) and boxing gloves, sparring and chanting, "We fight for you!" all along the parade route. Aside from the all moist tortillas thrown at us, we had a ball. Participants from around the state were able to meet each other face-to-face and deduct their travel expenses, while doing public relations work for our organization.

- Speaking of travel, Doctors without Borders (http://www.doctorswithoutborders.org) needs more than just doctors and nurses. They can use good administrators and people with language skills, especially French and Arabic.

- As another fun place to volunteer, your local music center or philharmonic venues need volunteers to take tickets, be ushers, work food service, and more. You will get to see most of the performance for free and meet all kinds of interesting people, both volunteers and guests.

- Like animals? Zoos and animal sanctuaries can use your help. Internet search engines are marvelous tools to help you find places that care for your favorite land, sea, and air creatures.

- Add your own ideas. The volunteer opportunities are limited only by your imagination. To meet writers, artists, and celebrities, find out which charities they run, or those in which they actively participate. You can also search the web for local organizations that have put out the call for volunteers. Here's one: https://www.volunteermatch.org.

Tip #158:

An amazing resource for exempt organization administrators and volunteers. Have you ever heard of TechSoup (http://www.techsoup.org)? Wow! This is a great place to get free, or seriously discounted, software, refurbished computers, tools, and supplies for your entity. You can find entire suites from Microsoft, Intuit, Cisco, GoDaddy, NetSuite, Norton, and many, many more big name vendors. It's free to register. So don't overlook this valuable resource. You will find more resources, like TechSoup and other goodies, at the Foundation Center (http://foundationcenter.org/gainknowledge/nonprofit links). Remember, as an exempt organization, you have access to government grants, cable television time, corporation foundation grants, and lots more free money—if you know where to find it.

Tip #159:

Start your own. Yes, if you have a passion and time, why not start your own nonprofit organization? Remember the Shelters for Israel ladies (Tip #137)? What do you love to do? With whom do you love to spend your time? Why give your charitable dollars to someone who will spend big chunks on high salaries for executives? (For instance, the United Way Worldwide raised about $78 million in 2013 and spent more than $23 million in salaries and compensation with more than $4 million going to executives in various forms of compensation: http://990s.foundationcenter.org/990_pdf_archive/131/131635294/131635294_201312_990.pdf?_ga=1.209184212.7586 187.1446561556.) How do you start your own charity or association? Well, I'll admit that it's not very easy. You will need the help of a tax professional who is experienced setting them up. It all starts with two things:

- A solid business plan where you define your mission, how you plan to achieve your goal, whether you will fund it all or raise funds, how you will get volunteers to participate, and who you will be serving.
- A tax form. Use one of these forms—Form 1023 (1023-EZ) or Form 1024 (https://www.irs.gov/Charities-&-Non-Profits/Applying-for-Tax-Exempt-Status).

Incidentally, the IRS has an amazingly detailed website to walk you through the entire process, including online training materials (https://www.irs.gov/Charities-&-Non-Profits). You will find an entire area about the Life Cycle of an Exempt Organization that can take you from conception, to inception, to operation of your organization (https://www.irs.gov/Charities-&-Non-Profits/Life -Cycle-of-an-Exempt-Organization).

CHAPTER 11

Retirement Tax Issues for the Young at Heart

M Y GOOD FRIEND WOLFGANG is about to turn seventy years old. He has been running his own business, a school, for more than forty years. Wolfgang has savings and he collects Social Security. Essentially, he is in good shape financially. Until you scratch the surface. Then you learn that he is reluctant to take vacations for more than a week or so because he will lose students and the related stream of income. Wolfgang made a very interesting comment: "If I knew that I would live for a specific number of additional years, I would be quite relaxed about taking time off and taking vacations. Because I would know exactly how to budget my money to last for those finite years. Heck, I might even stop working altogether." His big concern is that his father is in his mid-nineties and is apt to live for many more years. So Wolfgang needs to build savings to carry him through twenty or more years, some of which will be potentially unproductive years.

He makes an excellent point for all of us. If we had a functioning crystal ball, it would be supremely simple to know exactly how much to save and how much money we can spend enjoying the moment! After all, members of our Baby Boomer generation who are reading this right now, clearly did not "Live fast, die young, and leave a beautiful corpse" (http://quoteinvestigator .com/2013/01/31/live-fast). We're still here. Some of us are active, vital, and pursuing life's pleasures with even more gusto than we did in our thirties and forties. So what's a person to do?

Tip #160:

Start setting aside money toward retirement as soon as you can. Your most obvious choices are:

- Open a savings account.
- Use an IRA—Individual Retirement Account with deductible contributions.
- Use a Roth IRA—Individual Retirement Account with non-deductible contributions now—but no taxes when you retire.
- Use one of the many retirement plans offered at work. See what your employer has to offer.
  - Some employers offer to match your contributions—definitely invest as much as you can in those plans. At least invest as much as your employer will match.
  - Some employers offer a Roth option to their retirement plans. That means you won't get a deduction when you invest. You will get the benefits when you retire. (That's called delayed gratification.)
- Buy US Savings Bonds.

- Invest in stocks, bonds, or securities.

- Buy a whole life insurance policy.

- Invest in real estate.

- Or, if you have a working crystal ball and know what will increase in value—invest in that!

Tip #161:

What do the Roth and regular IRA have in common? Both have the same annual contribution limits.

- Presently for 2015 and 2016, the limits are $5,500 per person, or $6,500 if your age is fifty or over (https://www .irs.gov/Retirement-Plans/Plan-Participant,-Employee/ Retirement-Topics-IRA-Contribution-Limits).

- Your contributions to all IRAs are limited to your earned income.

- Even though your spouse is not working, you may contribute to a spousal IRA (Roth or regular), as long as the total of all your IRA contributions do not exceed your earned income.

- Earned income consists of the total of all your wages and your self-employment profits, which can come from your Schedule C or your general partnership income from a Form 1065 (reported on Schedule E, page 2).

- If you have self-employed losses that wipe out your self-employment income, you won't be able to make any IRA contributions.

- All earnings inside the plans grow tax-free.

- You are permitted to roll over balances from your other IRAs or pension plans into any of your IRA accounts, Roth or regular, without paying any early withdrawal penalties. (Rolling to a Roth will generate taxes.)

- You may roll over the money from an existing IRA or Roth IRA to another investment house only once per year (newly defined rule: https://www.irs.gov/Retirement-Plans/IRA -One-Rollover-Per-Year-Rule). When you do make a roll- over, if the funds are not transferred directly from the first IRA account to the new (or second) account, you must fin- ish moving the money within sixty days. Not two months. *Sixty days*! If you miss the deadline, the entire amount of the rollover becomes taxable immediately. Folks who are under age 59½ face all those nasty early withdrawal penal- ties (unless they meet certain exceptions).

- Yes, you are permitted to establish self-directed IRAs. But they are very expensive and complicated and can easily end up being disallowed, which means that everything in the account can become instantly taxable.

- You may draw your money out when you reach age 59½ with- out facing early withdrawal penalties. If you take the money earlier, you will face an IRS penalty for 10 percent of the tax- able balance plus whatever your state charges as a penalty.

Sounds good so far. So what are the differences?

Tip #162:

With a regular IRA, you get to deduct your contribution in the year you make the contribution. So you get an immediate tax benefit, or instant gratification. When you pull money out of your IRA, all your distribution is taxable. Why? You got a tax deduction for your original contribution—and all the earnings grew tax-free. So none of the money in the account has ever been taxed. This is especially important to understand when it comes to estate planning. Whoever inherits your IRA will also pay tax on the full balance in the account. Unlike other assets you might own at death, IRAs do not get special treatment. And remember, if you are covered by a retirement plan at work, your IRA deduction is limited based on the amount of your MAGI. You can find the most recent limits at the IRS website (https://www.irs.gov/Retirement-Plans/IRA-Deduction-Limits).

Tip #163:

But, you say, you *did* pay tax on some of your IRA contributions! What then? First of all, under what conditions might you have paid tax?

- Your income was too high to qualify for a deductible contribution but you contributed anyway. Keep track of those amounts on Form 8606 (https://www.irs.gov/pub/irs-prior/f8606-2014.pdf). That way, you, your heirs, and the IRS will know how much of your contribution was made with after-tax dollars.

- You live in a state that has (or had) a lower IRA contribution allowance than the IRS permits. While all your IRS contributions might have been deducted, you might have made nondeductible contributions on the state level. If the state doesn't have a form that lets you track this number, keep a worksheet in a permanent file that allows you to track the numbers. Let your tax pro, your estate attorney, and key members of your family know about this worksheet. For instance, California has a Publication 1005 which helps identify the basis differences for years when California had lower contribution limits (https://www.ftb.ca.gov/forms/2013/13_1005.pdf). What does your state have to help you?

Tip #164:

If you don't get a deduction for your Roth IRA contribution, what is the Roth IRA for? This is a perfect savings vehicle for people with long-term vision. You can stash away money, little by little, every year. Although you pay taxes on the money you deposit, you don't pay taxes on the earnings. However, you must leave the funds in the Roth IRA for five years before tapping it. The Roth IRA contributions are limited if your earnings are too high. Look up the MAGI earnings limits on the IRS website (https://www.irs.gov/Retirement-Plans/Roth-IRAs). Ah, but here are the rewards! When you finally retire, none of the money you draw out is taxable. You do not have to take any of those pesky Required Minimum Distributions (RMDs) at age 70½ (See Tip #166). When you die, no matter how much money is in the Roth account, none of it will be taxable to your heirs. Isn't that a terrific benefit? In fact, some 401(k) plans at work allow you make part of your contributions to a Roth 401(k) account. Remember how earlier I mentioned that you can roll over your pension balances to the Roth account? Yes, you can do this. And if you plan the rollovers properly, you can move the money while paying just a little tax on each rollover.

Tip #165:

Which is better, a regular IRA or a Roth IRA? That's a great question. And the answer depends on your income and asset level while you are working and when you retire.

- For people who expect to have very low levels of income when they retire, the regular IRA is better for them. Especially since they get that very valuable tax break in the year they make the IRA contribution. They probably won't build up hundreds of thousands of dollars in their IRA. They will probably end up using all the money in their lifetimes.

- The Roth is the perfect account for folks who expect to be in a higher tax bracket when they retire than when they were working. Believe it or not, I have seen this happen.

- For instance, meet my favorite Rabbi's wife, let's call her Janice. During the Rabbi's lifetime, he wasn't concerned about his earnings and gave away practically everything to help other people. As a result, contributions were high and taxable income was low. When he died, his Rabbi's pension was generous and Janice was able to collect Social Security. Since her time wasn't occupied taking care of all her rabbinical wifely duties, Janice was able to build a business teaching adults and children to get ready to present their Bar Mitzvah Bible portions. She had all this money pouring in. But her house was paid off, with a low property tax. As a result, Janice was able to save a lot of money. Some of it ended up in IRAs, some in investments. (Even after a very long and sad bout with Alzheimer's, there was still quite a bit of tax-free money left over for the children.)

- Janice isn't the only retiree I have known whose income has increased substantially after retirement. For folks with vision who know this is coming, stashing money into the Roth IRA is a great idea. One of my Enrolled Agent friends, Doug Thorburn in Northridge, California, spent several years working out the best plan to help his clients convert their other retirement assets to Roth IRAs. Doug developed some very sophisticated computational tools to determine the optimum amount to convert each year.

- Life doesn't always work out as planned, so he also had to learn how to recharacterize some of those annual conversions and move them back into IRA accounts. Ah, the problem with conversions. When you move the money too early in the year, you sometimes end up earning too much money that year, which makes the conversion much more expensive than you had intended (https://www.irs.gov/ Retirement-Plans/Roth-IRAs). The good news is you can often undo (recharacterize the conversion), as long as you do this by April 15.

- I had several clients who loved to fund Roth IRAs in January so the money would grow tax-free all year. The only problem was that their earnings were generally too high to qualify them for Roth IRAs. They would have two choices: withdraw the money or move it and recharacterize the funds into their regular IRA account. As a result, I encourage my eager-beaver, money-savvy clients to wait to fund Roth IRA accounts until November. That way you will know how much your earnings are for most of the year and have an idea of how much bonus to expect. (Or wait until March of the following year when all the numbers are in.)

Tip #166:

We mentioned RMDs a moment ago. What the heck are they? Well, they affect seniors age 70½ and older and their Required Minimum Distributions (RMDs). What is an RMD (https://www.irs.gov/Retirement-Plans/Plan-Participant ,-Employee/Retirement-Topics-Required-Minimum-Distributions -%28RMDs%29)? This is the least (minimum) amount of money you are required to withdraw from your IRAs and retirement accounts every year once you reach the ripe old age of 70½— give or take a few months. After all, you've been stashing away all this money for years, perhaps decades, without paying any taxes at all. Now Uncle Sam wants his cut.

Tip #167:

Timing. When must you start taking the distributions? You must take the first distribution by April 1 of the year after you reach age 70½. You have a little leeway. It doesn't need to be *the* year you turn age 70½. That's the good news. The bad news is—actually, there are three pieces of bad news:

1. Getting this extra time means that people put off taking the distribution and forget. Forgetting is expensive.

2. The penalty for not taking a distribution is 50 percent of the amount that should have been distributed.

3. If you wait until the April 1 of the following year, you must take two distributions during that year. One for the year you turned 70½, and the second one for the year in which you are age 71.

Tip #168:

Legitimate delay for RMD. If you are still working for the company where you have your retirement account in the year you turn 70½, you can put off taking the first distribution from that account until you retire from that company. Retirement accounts that qualify for this delay include 401(k)s, profit-sharing, 403(b)s, or other defined contribution plans. But you will have to take a distribution from that account in the year you retire. *Note: You must still take all the required distributions from your IRAs and other retirement accounts.*

Tip #169:

Distributions from *all* accounts? No, you don't need to take a distribution from each and every account you have. You may add up the value of all the accounts and compute the overall

RMD. Then you may choose to draw that year's distribution from one account, or several, as long as you draw at least the minimum amount. Naturally, you may withdraw more—just not less. Use this IRS worksheet to determine how much you must withdraw based on your age (https://www.irs.gov/pub/irs-tege/uniform_rmd_wksht.pdf). Do this each year, since account balances change based on investment returns.

Tip #170:

Reduce your IRA and retirement account balances as quickly as you can. The balance in your previously untaxed retirement accounts will be fully taxable to your heirs. So draw out more than the minimum amount if you can do that without raising your tax bill or moving up to a higher tax bracket.

Tip #171:

No RMD required. If all your retirement funds are in Roth IRAs, you don't have to worry about taking any distributions at all. So, as you draw the money from your other retirement accounts, if you don't need the cash this year, roll the funds into your Roth IRA. You will pay tax on those distributions and make the IRS happy, but the funds rolled into your Roth IRA can continue to grow tax-free. You can use the money anytime you like without paying taxes when you take the money (as long as the Roth IRA has been open for at least five years). And your heirs will get all that money tax-free as well.

Tip #172:

Avoid taxes on your RMD altogether. Make a nondeductible charitable contribution to your favorite charity of up to $100,000. Why would you want to make a $100,000 nondeductible donation? For several years, we have had a special provision in the Internal Revenue Code allowing senior citizens to make donations directly from their IRA accounts to the charity or charities of their choice (https://www.irs.gov/Retirement-Plans/Charitable-Donations-from-IRAs). This was targeted at folks ages 70½ or above who faced taking required minimum deposits (RMDs) from their retirement accounts or face hefty penalties. This option requires that the withdrawal is transferred directly to the charity (called a Qualified Direct Transfer, or QDT). If that is done properly, the senior gets two visible benefits and loses one benefit:

Benefit 1—They can count this draw as their RMD for the year.

Benefit 2—They don't have to pay taxes on the amount they have withdrawn and sent to the charity.

Drawback—They don't get to claim the charitable contribution deduction for this donation.

Tip #173:

Six more reasons for this nondeductible contribution. Here are the (sort of) intangible benefits:

1. This can be a terrific benefit for someone whose draw might otherwise cause their Social Security income to become taxable. An RMD of $5,000 might end up costing the taxpayer several thousand dollars in taxes because it causes Social Security income to become taxable, too, raising the AGI.

2. This can keep someone out of Alternative Minimum Tax (AMT) territory. As your income rises, you could face AMT.

3. Not adding the RMD to income keeps the AGI lower, so a variety of credits and deductions are not lost.

4. This makes it possible to keep estimated taxes lower during the year.

5. For people who tithe anyway, and couldn't otherwise use the deduction, this lets you keep tithing and hold your head up in the community as a generous donor.

6. By distributing much more money from your retirement than the minimum requirement, you can deplete this taxable asset without paying taxes on the draws.

In other words, this provision carries a lot of worthwhile benefits to the taxpayer. (There are probably several benefits I haven't even touched upon.)

Tip #174:

Warning: if this is such a great deal, why do I say "we have *had* a special provision?" Because this is another of those political footballs Congress likes to toss around each year. In some years (2012 and 2013), they didn't renew this provision until a month or two after the close of the tax year. For 2014, they renewed this provision around December 19, 2014, giving seniors days to make these transfers. As we write this, Congress still hasn't renewed this for 2015. So why do I bother even mentioning it? Because they usually do renew it.

Note: This has been made a permanent part of the Internal Revenue Code as Section 112 of the PATH Act of 2015. Please see Bonus Tip #270 for more details.

Tip #175:

Hooray! Congress has made this provision permanent. Since you like to make charitable contributions, make the donation.

You have nothing to lose, since you must take the minimum distribution anyway. Here are two ways to take advantage of this:

- Wait until December to take your RMD, so you can keep the earnings on these funds for the year.
- Take the distribution earlier in the year and have it sent directly to your charity.
  - You will get the deduction for your charitable contribution and you will pay tax on the distribution you had to take anyway.

Regardless, you will have drawn enough money to cover your RMD. Either way—you win!

Tip #176:

Understand when SS benefits and Equivalent Railroad Retirement Benefits are not taxable. *Note: Anytime you see anything about Social Security in this book, the information also covers "Equivalent Railroad Retirement Benefits."* When all your income comes from the Social Security Administration, none of the benefits are taxable. This applies to seniors, folks on Social Security Disability, and children collecting survivor's benefits after a parent has died. There is no tax when you are single (S), the head of household (HOH), the qualifying widow or widower (QW) with a dependent child, or married individuals filing separately if all your income, plus half the Social Security income, stays below $25,000. For married couples filing jointly, the limit is $32,000. Beware: when married couples live together and file separately (MFS), 85 percent of their Social Security benefits are taxed immediately. There is no exclusion for MFS.

Tip #177:

When your income is higher than the Social Security limits, what is the tax effect? When income rises above that, suddenly up to 85 percent of the SS income becomes taxable. You can use the IRS worksheets (they have examples) in Publication 915 to figure out how much of your benefits will be taxable (https://www.irs.gov/publications/p915/ar02.html). However, your tax software will also have tools to make these computations. In fact, it might just be easier to log into some live tax software and enter your income and Social Security benefits to see exactly where you stand.

Tip #178:

Let's look at a tangible effect of adding RMDs or retirement rollovers to your AGI when you're collecting Social Security. You are married. The two of you collect a total of $23,000 from Social Security. Your interest income is $5,000. Your total AGI is $5,000 because none of your Social Security income is taxable. Now let's add an RMD of $15,000. Good news! No tax effect because half of your Social Security benefits ($11,500) plus your additional income are still less than $32,000. That means you can either draw this money or move it to a Roth IRA. What happens if you take $30,000? Adding this $15,000 to your income means that $8,125 of your Social Security benefits becomes taxable. So adding $15,000 actually means raising your income by $23,125. The good news is, after the standard deduction and personal exemptions for seniors, your taxable income is low enough that you end up paying less than $2,000 for the $30,000 you drew from your retirement account. That's less than 7 percent (plus whatever your state charges). Raising the distribution to $50,000 however, means $19,550, or 85 percent, of your Social Security benefits are taxable (the maximum level). You end up paying nearly $7,000 in IRS taxes (plus state taxes) on that $50,000. Actually, this is still not bad because you're paying less than 14 percent of the distribution.

- Do you see how you can test numbers in your live account to see what the real tax effect will be? Remember, those live tax software accounts are free to play around in. You only pay when you actually file a tax return . . . though some of the services will charge you if you print the forms.
- Based on your comfort level with respect to paying no taxes or, say, up to a 15 percent tax rate, you can find the ideal amount of distributions to draw from your taxable retirement accounts.
- This can give you a good way to determine the highest amount to draw from all your taxable IRAs and pensions— or even how much you can afford to produce when it comes to capital gains.
- Naturally, by working with an experienced tax professional, you can get even more guidance on how to manage the flow of funds to get the lowest tax hit on the most cash.

Tip #179:

Social Security Form SSA-1099 also contains fees for Medicare benefits. Those amounts are deductible as health insurance costs. In fact, if you are self-employed, you are entitled to take these into account for your self-employed health insurance deduction.

Tip #180:

Lump sum payments from Social Security. If you know any-one who ever applied for Social Security Disability, you know they got rejected. Probably at least two to three times before they finally got approved. This practice is shameful and harmful on the part of the Social Security Administration (SSA). People who cannot work and desperately need money to live on don't get money for years, often losing their homes or other security as they wipe out savings and run up debt. This also means that the applicant often ends up hiring an attorney to help get their claim approved—and loses 35–50 percent of their benefit after all fees and cost reimbursements are deducted. Yet they must pay tax on all the money they received, right? The taxable part of this is not as bad as you think. (Though it doesn't make up for the havoc caused before approval.)

1. When the SSA finally approves the claim, they pay you based on the date of your original claim. So you will get three to four years of benefits all at one time. Yes, you must report the entire amount in the year you get the money.

2. You must report the gross amount of your award even though your attorney gets that large chunk. Deduct the attorney's fees and costs on Schedule A as a Miscella-neous Itemized Deduction reduced by 2 percent of your AGI (https://www.irs.gov/publications/p529/ar02.html).

3. There is a special computation (and worksheet) you can use that treats the money as though you received it over several years (https://www.irs.gov/publications/p915/ar02 .html#en_US_2014_publink100097893). If you are using commercial tax return software and can't figure out how to get the program to do this, call their tech support line. I guarantee that they have all built this into their systems. If

you cannot figure it out, or don't have the patience, take it to a tax pro for the year in which you get this settlement. It will be well worth it to end up paying less tax.

Tip #181:

You're finally collecting Social Security Disability Income (SSDI), but you can't live on it. Are you allowed to do any work at all to supplement the income? Yes you are! You must earn less than $1,090 per month ($1,820 if you are blind) in 2015. Visit https://www.socialsecurity.gov/planners/disability/dwork2 .html to see what the limits are in the current year (the year in which you read this).

Tip #182:

You're not disabled, but you're collecting Social Security before you reach your full retirement age of 66, or . . . Be careful when you start collecting early. Most people cannot live on their SS benefits, so they still have to work to supplement those Social Security checks (especially after they deduct Medicare payments). What is the maximum amount you are allowed to earn? For 2015 and 2016, you may earn up to $15,720 in wages or net self-employment income. (Use this chart to look up later years: https://www.ssa.gov/oact/cola/ rtea.html.) When you earn any more than that, you must pay back the good old Social Security Administration to the tune of $1 for every $2 dollars you earn past this limit. This is bad for at least two reasons:

- If you don't pay the money back in the same year that you received it, you will include the full amount of SS benefits in your income—even though you will have to repay some of it in the following year.

- You started collecting SS benefits early, so you have locked in a lower monthly benefit than you would have gotten if had you waited until age 66, or your minimum Social Security retirement age. And you now have to repay some of those lower benefits you have. Doesn't this seem like such a waste?

So review your needs carefully before applying early. Don't apply for Social Security benefits if you cannot afford to live on them and are still healthy enough to earn more than the allowable limits.

Tip #183:

When don't you have to pay anything back? This will make you furious if you aren't wealthy enough to qualify. People who don't need to work, people who have investment income (any kind at all—interest, dividends, rentals, capital gains, pensions, etc.), can receive an unlimited amount of investment income while collecting SS benefits early. Can you see the inequity in this? Sooner or later, some working stiff will refuse to pay this back and will take the whole issue to court until it reaches the Supreme Court. Surely this will fall under one discrimination law or another. I can see this rule being struck down someday. But for now, start your savings program early so you can be among those who have investment income.

Tip #184:

Can you control your earned income? Yes you can. Many years ago I was a speaker at a CPA dinner meeting. One of the CPAs there was saying that she had just started to collect her Social Security benefits early. Because, clearly, she was still working, I asked about the repayment requirement. She said she doesn't have to worry about that. Her CPA practice was in an

S corporation. She could keep her wages under the earnings limit set by the SSA, and all the rest of her profits would come to her as dividends. This strategy would also work with a C corporation. It won't work in a partnership. But beware if you have been operating a business and continue to do so. If you continue to work as much as before, but your earned income (wages) suddenly drops and becomes dividends, you can expect an audit. And you can expect to lose that audit, with respect to the level of wages. So don't bring yourself to the attention of the IRS needlessly.

Tip #185:

We mentioned that sometimes you get too much money from Social Security and have to pay it back. There are four ways to deal with this repayment:

1. If the repayment is less than the benefits you're still getting, you don't need to do anything. The SSA-1099 for the year in which you make the repayments will show the net benefits in box 5. You will only pick up that amount on your tax return. Easy peasy.

2. Your repayments are more than the benefits you receive. The amount in box 5 is negative and it is $3,000 or less. You must deduct that amount as a Miscellaneous Itemized Deduction, reduced by 2 percent of your AGI.

3. Suppose the repayment amount in box 5 shows a negative number that is more than $3,000. In that case, you are allowed to deduct it on Schedule A. In this case, you won't have to reduce it by that nasty 2 percent of AGI. You would put this on a different line—line 28 instead of line 23.

4. But when the amount is more than $3,000, you have another option. Remember when we talked about the "claim of right" rules? Read Tip #269, where we explain "claim of

right," to learn how to get a tax credit instead of a deduction. Your best bet is to try both ways. (Yes, I know it's a pain!) Generally, the more complicated credit computation will give you more money back. It boils down to refiguring your income as if the money had been paid back in the year it was received. You just won't actually have to amend that prior-year return. You may need some help with this. (Warning: Not all tax pros understand how to deal with this concept. So if you do go to a pro, ask them if they have ever prepared a return with a "claim of right" computation.)

Tip #186:

We talked about getting too much Social Security income, but what if you don't have enough? There are lots of people who worked for themselves, cleverly showing the lowest possible taxable profits to keep their taxes low. Or they came to the United States later in life. Perhaps they worked for employers who did not participate in the Social Security system. Suddenly, they look up and realize they haven't worked in the Social Security system for the full forty quarters (ten years). What do they need to do to catch up? It's time to get a job with an employer who pays into the system, or start a business where you have self-employment profits. The wages or profits must be at least $5,040 per year ($1260 per quarter). You can look up the annual minimum earnings requirement on the Social Security website (https://www.socialsecurity.gov/oact/cola/QC.html).

Tip #187:

Suppose you are, and have been, legitimately self-employed, but your taxable profits just don't reach that level. Is there something you can do? You bet there is. Take a look at Part II of Schedule SE's Schedule B (https://www.irs.gov/pub/irs-pdf/

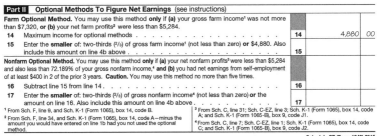

Part II   Optional Methods To Figure Net Earnings (see instructions)

Farm Optional Method. You may use this method **only if (a)** your gross farm income[1] was not more than $7,320, **or (b)** your net farm profits[2] were less than $5,284.

14	Maximum income for optional methods	**14**	4,880	00
15	Enter the **smaller** of: two-thirds (²/₃) of gross farm income[1] (not less than zero) **or** $4,880. Also include this amount on line 4b above	**15**	

Nonfarm Optional Method. You may use this method **only if (a)** your net nonfarm profits[3] were less than $5,284 and also less than 72.189% of your gross nonfarm income,[4] **and (b)** you had net earnings from self-employment of at least $400 in 2 of the prior 3 years. **Caution.** You may use this method no more than five times.

16	Subtract line 15 from line 14	**16**	
17	Enter the **smaller** of: two-thirds (²/₃) of gross nonfarm income[4] (not less than zero) **or** the amount on line 16. Also include this amount on line 4b above	**17**	

[1] From Sch. F, line 9, and Sch. K-1 (Form 1065), box 14, code B.
[2] From Sch. F, line 34, and Sch. K-1 (Form 1065), box 14, code A—minus the amount you would have entered on line 1b had you not used the optional method.
[3] From Sch. C, line 31; Sch. C-EZ, line 3; Sch. K-1 (Form 1065), box 14, code A; and Sch. K-1 (Form 1065-B), box 9, code J1.
[4] From Sch. C, line 7; Sch. C-EZ, line 1; Sch. K-1 (Form 1065), box 14, code C; and Sch. K-1 (Form 1065-B), box 9, code J2.

Schedule SE (Form 1040) 2015

f1040sse.pdf). It's on the bottom of the second page of this form. There are two "Optional Methods"—one for farmers, and one for other businesses (nonfarm). When your profits are too low, you have the option of paying the higher amount of self-employment taxes to ensure that you meet the Social Security Administration's forty-quarter earnings requirement. Most people either overlook it or simply don't understand it and never ask. Take a look and see what I mean: https://www.irs.gov/pub/irs-pdf/f1040sse.pdf.

Tip #188:

OK, you do have your forty quarters in, but the income isn't very high. How can you raise the income in your Social Security account? Wow. That is a great question. OK, here are some ideas:

- Get a new job. I find that people who have held the same job for ten years or more often aren't valued as much as new employees (at least, not in terms of compensation). Foolishly, companies often pay new hires more than current employees. So start looking at your company's competitors to see where you would be more valuable.
  - A story: I used to work as a headhunter, recruiting professionals in the financial and computer fields. Pacific

Mutual was looking for an investment programmer with particular skills and, at the time, they were willing to pay up to $100,000 for the position. I located and spoke to the five top programmers in the industry. (This was so specialized that these were the only guys doing it.) Not a single one would move for less than $150,000. (They were all earning more than $100,000 already.) But! I knew of a programmer (a classmate of mine in my MBA program) who happened to have exactly the skills that Pacific Mutual was seeking. In fact, he was developing just such a system for an investment manager. He was only earning about $50,000. They could afford him—probably for about $75,000, maybe even less. The only problem? He was already an employee of Pacific Mutual. He was developing the software for one of their own fund managers. No, they wouldn't pay me a commission for him. OK, I can live with that. After all, he's a good friend. But would they promote him to the position and give him a raise? No. They would not give that much of a raise to someone inside their own company. See what I mean? Start shopping around. (Chuck did, and he worked for some of the top corporations in the country, earning ever more on each move.)

• Get a second job. The additional income will be added to the earnings for your regular job, thereby showing that you are earning substantially more each year.

• Start a business—even if it's on the side. Follow your passion. So many people who start a blog, or sell their handicrafts, or start to provide a service start making more money than they had ever imagined. After all, even a profit of $10,000 can increase your Social Security benefits over your lifetime. (Heck, I have seen people go online and start businesses, slowly and painstakingly, and end up as millionaires. While it may not happen to you, you might just increase your income by $50,000 or more per year.)

- Of course, the passive alternative. Don't start collecting Social Security early (age 62), or at your regular retirement age (age 67 and above). Wait until you are age 70 to get a higher payout each month. This is worth doing if your family has a history of living into their late eighties or nineties and you don't have any deadly or debilitating medical issues.

Tip #189:

For how long must you earn the additional income in order to raise your Social Security benefits? Well, it all depends on your overall earnings history.

- The Social Security Administration looks at your highest 35 years of earnings. (This was a shock to me, since it used to be the last 10 years. Now I have to scramble to increase my own earnings before I retire.) They first recompute your annual earnings to index them for inflation, then add up the earnings for the 35 years with the highest numbers and divide by 35 years. You can see an example here. Look at the "Indexed Earnings" column. See how $8,070 in 1975 translates to $41,971 in 2015 (https://www.ssa.gov/oact/progdata/retirebenefit1.html)?

- To see where you stand, start by requesting your report from the Social Security Administration. You can do this online, or you can file a Form SSA-7004 to get a free copy (https://secure.ssa.gov/RIL/SiView.do; https://www.socialsecurity.gov/myaccount/materials/pdfs/SSA-7004.pdf). This can take several weeks, so try the online option. I just tried the online version—it took a couple of minutes. What took longer? I lost over an hour, fascinated with the data I found in my account. (Incidentally, I requested the written report while I was online and it arrived in less than a week.)

- Now that you have the information, add up your 35 highest earnings years and see what the average is. How much should you raise your income each year to increase the benefit? Use the benefit calculators (particularly the Online Calculator) that the SSA provides to help you see what happens when your income increases (https://www.socialsecurity.gov/planners/benefitcalculators.html). This will help you decide if it's worth it to sacrifice the irreplaceable precious hours you have with your family and friends.

  - Someone wrote to TaxMama trying to decide if it was worthwhile to reduce her wages by using a Flexible Spending Account or if it would reduce her Social Security benefit when she would retire in about two to three years. Answering her question led me to the resources I just gave you. Yes, your questions help me learn!

Tip #190:

We've been talking about putting money away for retirement, but what about using some of the money before you retire? Rumor has it that you can draw out money as a down payment on your home or to pay education expenses without paying taxes. *False*! Big time false! So the best tip I can give you is: before you ever take money out of any account that is meant to be a retirement account, invest in two hours with your tax professional. Period.

Let's look at some of the reasons for this.

Tip #191:

When you draw money out any retirement account (except a Roth-type account), there will always be taxes. When you draw the money out before you reach age 59½, there are ways to avoid the 10 percent early withdrawal penalties that the IRS assesses, plus the state penalties. But these exceptions only work if you draw the money out of an IRA. When you draw the money from your 401(k) or other pension plan, everything is still subject to penalties. I see people do this all the time and it breaks my heart. Why? Because they don't ask TaxMama or anyone else until after they've drawn the money and it's too late to roll the funds back in and fix the problem. So the second tip about drawing money from retirement accounts is: move the money you will need to an IRA account. Yes, it is a pain to go through the process. But if you don't, you will waste the money on penalties, needlessly.

Tip #192:

Add about 25 percent to your draw. Heck, add 25 percent plus your state tax rate. What am I talking about? You've moved the money you will need to your IRA, so now what's the problem? Well, the draw will still face full taxation for both the IRS and your state. In fact, the administrator is required to withhold 20 percent of your distribution and to send it to the IRS. So right off the bat you're only going to get 80 percent of the money you are expecting. The rest goes to your IRS account to pay some of your estimated taxes. Does that mean you will owe nothing in April, at least? No? Once the full amount of your draw is added to your wages, you will probably end up owing more than 20 percent. So here you are, drawing this money and only getting 80 percent of it, but you are paying taxes on 100 percent of the money—money you never got. What am I trying to tell you? The third important IRA draw tip is this: even without the penalties, this is not a good deal. By the time all the tax issues are taken into account, you end up paying around 30–40 percent in taxes on the net cash you receive. So if there is a way to get the money elsewhere . . . do it. Even credit cards are cheaper than drawing money out of your IRA or retirement account. Don't believe me? Run the numbers in advance.

Tip #193:

OK, you're going to do this anyway. So where is the list of draws you can take while you're still young that won't cost you an early withdrawal penalty? Good news. After years of pestering the IRS to show the information cleanly and simply, they finally did. And it's a really nice table on this page on their Retirement-Plans website (https://www.irs.gov/Retirement -Plans/Plan-Participant,-Employee/Retirement-Topics---Tax -on-Early-Distributions). *Note: I am still bugging them to add the code number or letter that you will need to use on line 2, Form 5329 (https://www.irs.gov/pub/irs-pdf/f5329.pdf). After all, to you, the Internal Revenue Code section is meaningless. What you need to see on that page is the form number to use this information on and the code number for the specific exclusion from the penalty.*

Tip #194:

What are the most commonly used exceptions? There is so much information in this one area that I can easily teach a four-hour class on it all. So, please, for more details, read the instructions to Form 5329 and work with a tax pro (https://www.irs .gov/pub/irs-pdf/i5329.pdf). Meanwhile, here are some of the more commonly used, or useful, exceptions to the penalties:

- Code 03: Total and permanent disability. This must be provable with a letter from a doctor. A temporary disability does not qualify.
- Code 04: Death. Need I say more?

- Code 06: Qualified Domestic Relations Order (QDRO). Ironically, this distribution may *not* come from an IRA. It may only come from a qualified retirement plan. This may only be used in a divorce to split the retirement account by order of a court.

- Code 08: Funds are used to pay for qualified education expenses. If you have scholarships, grants, or Coverdell ESA funds, make sure you have enough educational expenses to cover this draw as well.

- Code 09: $10,000 for the down payment on a first home. (You may not have owned a home for at least three years.) *Note: To draw out $20,000, you and your spouse must each draw up to $10,000 from your separate IRAs. You may not draw the $20,000 from one IRA just because you're married.*

Tip #195:

Beware the phantom income. One of the best ways to get your hands on money from your pension plan is to borrow from it. Not all companies make this available. But when they do, you are allowed to borrow up to 50 percent of the balance of your qualified retirement account, or up to $50,000 (whichever number is lower). The great part about this is that there are no tax consequences. There is no early withdrawal penalty. They don't hold back any of the funds to pay to the IRS for estimated taxes. So if you draw $50,000, you actually get $50,000—not 80 percent of that amount. And the fees are minimal, around $100 or so. Best of all, you pay yourself back at a very low interest rate. It's all good, right?

Nope. If you leave the company before you pay all the money back, you will have to pay taxes and possibly early withdrawal penalties on the unpaid balance. It doesn't matter if you were laid off, fired, or quit.

Be sure you know how much you owe before you leave so you can settle the account. Often, the plan administrator will give you three to six months to secure a loan so you can pay them back. But if you run out of time, you're toast! After all, if you still owe $30,000, you will be adding this to your income, which will probably push you into at least a 25 percent bracket (if you were not already there). Add the state taxes of about 10 percent. Then add the early withdrawal penalties of, say, 12.5 percent (IRS + California). You will need to come up with nearly 50 percent of that $30,000 in taxes and penalties. So be super diligent about finding a way to pay back your employer. At least if it's your decision to leave you have time to plan some strategy (like to request a huge hiring bonus from your new employer) to come up with the balance due.

Tip #196:

What is the best deal on the list but the least understood? Code 02, a series of substantially equal payments. This is the Internet millionaire provision. Yep, this is the provision that lets Internet mavens build up substantial retirement accounts, roll them over to IRAs, and start collecting their retirement benefits in their thirties instead of waiting until their sixties. It's called a Sec 72t election (https://www.irs.gov/Retirement-Plans/Retirement-Plans-FAQs-regarding-Substantially-Equal-Periodic-Payments). You basically turn your newly stuffed IRA into an annuity. You recalculate the withdrawals each year based on the growth or losses in the account. This is quite tricky, so work with a retirement professional who really, really, really understands the process well. Otherwise you will suddenly find yourself facing IRS and state withdrawal penalties on all the money you have drawn for years.

Tip #197:

This is a huge area and could probably fill a couple of books. In fact, I have spent more time on this chapter than any other chapter in the book. Yet I feel as if I have left out so very much. (I didn't even scratch the surface of self-directed IRAs.) So please, please, this is the one area of taxation where I want you to be a Tax Vigilante, or at least Tax Aware. Don't do anything in this chapter on your own. Getting good advice can save you thousands of dollars—and put more money into your pocket than you can imagine.

CHAPTER 12

Long-Term Savings and Retirement Tax Issues for the Very Young

MY FRIEND RITA BECAME an Enrolled Agent later in life. She was in her fifties when she started her tax practice, working out of her home. Many of her first clients were young people—college students and newlyweds who worked for fairly low wages. She gained a large following quickly. Why? Not because she got them high, unreasonable refunds. Her popularity soared because she taught these young people how to start saving money even when they didn't have much spare cash. How did she do it? First of all, Rita Veen, EA, is one of the most loving, focused women I know. She really cares and pays attention to her clients and their long-term needs. Second, Rita started setting her young clients up with three-month trial subscriptions to *The MoneyPaper* so they could learn some basic investment skills. (More about this in a moment.) A funny thing happened. The young folks started telling their parents and grandparents about Rita. Some of those adults were quite wealthy with complex tax issues. Because Rita honestly cared for her clients (and their children and grandchildren), it took no time at all to build up a healthy and wealthy client base. I care about you, too. So let's start with Rita's secret weapon— saving in tiny increments.

Tip #198:

It's never too early to start saving for retirement. A good time to start is when your baby is born. There are all kinds of ways to start build savings. All of them have advantages and disadvantages. But so does everything in life. The DRIP Investment site (it used to be the *MoneyPaper* magazine) shows how much security you can build up for your children with as little as $25 per month for 62 years (https://www.directinvesting .com/index.cfm). You start it and teach them to keep adding to it as soon as they are old enough to understand numbers.

Time VS. Money

Patient long-term investors will amass wealth by following the simple strategy that direct investment plans (DRIPs) make accessible to almost everyone.

Use our quick calculator below

Assuming a 10% average return over the long term, see how much your assets can grow over the years.

| $25 | / mo.   For | 62 | / yrs.

(Note: As you reduce the number of years, you must increase in the amount you invest in order to achieve a smiliar result)

Submit

Your investment would be worth: **$1,476,148.69**. Your cost was: **$18,655.00**
Click to see presumptions and calculations

Naturally, you can put the money into savings accounts, brokerage accounts, "dividend reinvestment programs" (DRIPs), or save up for US Savings Bonds. But if you want your children to learn secure investing, the DRIP site helps you find no-fee or low-fee DRIPs where you can buy the shares directly from the company, sometimes for as little as $10 or $25 (https://www.directinvesting.com/25_dollar_drips.cfm). Take a look their "kid's portfolio" (https://www.directinvesting.com/drip_learning_center/starter_portfolio.cfm?from=kids). In the past, they would include stocks that came with benefits. Now fewer companies offer them (http://www.wsj.com/articles/SB100014240 52702303330204579250763759331636). Disney used to offer shareholder discounts, Wrigley sent out packs of gum, Starbucks gave out gift cards—all gone! Kimberly Clark stockholders still get an annual gift box of goodies for about half the retail price (http://www.kcgiftbox.com/store/c/18-Gift-Box.aspx). Ford shareholders who can prove ownership get discounts on vehicle purchases. Some cruise lines offer onboard discounts. Berkshire-Hathaway shareholders who attend the stockholders' meetings can get a whole array of discounts and goodies in their meeting packet.

Tip #199:

Speaking of saving in small increments, there is a relatively new IRA you can set up, called myRA (https://myra.gov/how-it-works). It works a lot like a Roth IRA, which means you don't get a deduction for your contributions and will not pay tax when you draw the money at retirement (age 59½ or more).

- The main advantage is that once you open it, you may make deposits in teensy tiny increments, like $2. Of course, you may deposit more . . . but you don't have to.
- It costs nothing to open.

- You can fund it from your paycheck, if your boss participates in the program. Just set it up and forget it and you build up savings painlessly.

- Or you can fund it via direct deposit from your savings or checking account.

- You can even use your IRS tax refund to put money into your myRA. Just check the "savings account" box on your tax return or on Form 8888 and enter the account number.

- The annual contribution limit is the same as the limit for IRAs and Roth IRAs—$5,500 ($6,500 if you are age fifty or older) through December 31, 2016. Visit the IRS website for annual updates (https://www.irs.gov/Retirement -Plans/Plan-Participant,-Employee/Retirement-Topics -IRA-Contribution-Limits).

- The myRA is backed by the US Treasury and earns a higher rate of return than most small savings accounts—they claim it averaged 3.19 percent over the ten years ending in December 2014. As I write this, Bankrate.com is showing a return of .85 percent on the five-year certificate of deposit. *Five* years at less than 1 percent? *Wow!* In the weekly CD rates analysis on November 12, 2015, the one-year CD yields 0.27 percent while the five-year CD yields 0.85 percent. For a $100,000 deposit, the average one-year jumbo CD yield was 0.31 percent for the ninth straight week. The five-year jumbo yield was 0.89 percent for the second consecutive week. The average money market account yield was 0.09 percent for the fifty-seventh consecutive week (http://www .bankrate.com/cd.aspx). OK, the Federal Reserve raised the interest rate in December, for the first time in years. The returns increased by a small fraction. http://www.federal reserve.gov/newsevents/press/monetary/20151216a.htm.

- There are no fees!

- When your account reaches $15,000, you need to roll it over to a Roth IRA. Hopefully, by then, you can get a decent rate of return in the Roth IRA. In fact, if you see that you can get a better rate of return sooner, roll it over to your Roth IRA anytime you like.

- *Note: To learn how much your investment would be worth in the future, Google this phrase to find a calculator to help you—"future value of monthly deposit."*

Tip #200:

Coverdell Education Savings Accounts (ESA). This is another IRA-type account with no tax break when you fund it. This is often called the Education IRA (https://www.irs.gov/publications/ p970/ch07.html). Folks may contribute up to $2,000 per year into the ESA for each designated beneficiary as long as the contributor's Modified Adjusted Gross Income (MAGI) is less than certain annual limits, which change each year (https://www .irs.gov/publications/p970/ch07.html#en_US_2014_publink 1000178431). You may contribute to your offspring, your grandchildren, even the children of your employees or just for a friend. The purpose of this account is to set aside money to help fund a person's education someday. While there is no deduction for the contribution, the earnings in the account grow tax-free. So if you can find a stable investment that can generate a decent rate of return, these accounts can be a valuable way to grow college funds tax-free. If you don't have the skills or contacts to find secure investments paying more than a quarter of a percentage, skip it. Just put the money into a savings account for your child. It won't have any strings attached to the withdrawals. And the earnings will be low enough each year that the annual taxes will be insignificant, or there won't be any at all.

Tip #201:

Strings on the Coverdell ESA withdrawals. There are restrictions on how the money can be used. For this account, the restrictions are not too burdensome. Let's explore them:

- The educational institution must be "qualified." The IRS says, "This is any college, university, vocational school, or other postsecondary educational institution eligible to participate in a student aid program administered by the US Department of Education." It includes virtually all accredited public, nonprofit, and proprietary (privately owned profit-making) postsecondary institutions.

  ○ This includes certain overseas educational institutions.

  ○ Did you notice that this also includes "vocational" schools? You don't need to be a scholar to use these funds. You can train to become an auto mechanic, plumber, long-haul trucker, master chef, esthetician, hairdresser, dress designer, deep sea diver—or whatever your heart desires.

  ○ However, if the educational institution simply provides continuing professional education, or isn't accredited with the US Department of Education, you cannot use the ESA account funds for those schools.

- Eligible higher education expenses include:

  ○ Tuition and fees.

  ○ Books, supplies, and equipment, including computers and related supplies.

  ○ Room and board—either the actual amount charged by the school if the student is staying in school housing or the budget amount determined by the school's financial aid folks if the student is residing off campus.

- For special needs students, only those additional costs related to making it possible to enroll in and attend the school.
- *Surprise*! You can also use these funds for an eligible elementary or secondary school. This includes any public, private, or religious school that provides elementary or secondary education (kindergarten through grade twelve) as determined under state law.
  - Most people don't realize that the ESA is the only account that lets you use the savings for K-12 costs.
  - When you have friends, employers, and relatives funding these accounts, this is a great way to tap into the money to cover the high costs of private schools.
- Eligible K-12 education expenses include all the above, plus these additional costs:
  - academic tutoring
  - transportation
  - uniforms
  - extended daycare programs or other supplementary costs

Tip #202:

Coverdell ESA myth. The main drawback is that we may only deposit up to $2,000 per child, per year, no matter who provides the funds. Even if you start the account the year the child is born, by the time they turn 18 there will only be $36,000 in the account, plus the earnings. At 3 percent per year, that would be about $50,000 (http://www.hcuonline.com/HCU_Calc_Periodic Savings.html). That might be enough to cover higher education costs for a year or two. But if you use the funds for private school (K-12), the money would be depleted before it even earned any interest.

Periodic Deposit Calculator

This calculator will help you to determine the value of putting money away in to savings on a regular basis. **Note: Your actual amount saved my vary from these calculations.**	
To calculate the future value of a periodic investment, enter the beginning balance, the periodic dollar amount you plan to deposit, the deposit interval, the interest rate you expect to earn, and the number of years you expect to continue making monthly deposits, then click the "Compute" button.	

Enter the initial investment (optional):	2000
Enter the [Annual ⬍] deposit amount:	2000
Enter the annual interest rate: see our rates Enter 0.5% as 0.005	.03
Enter the number of years:	18
Compute Reset	
Future value:	$50,233.74
Interest earned:	$12,233.74

Tip #203:

No harm, no foul. Direct gifts of educational costs. Did you know that when you pay someone's education costs directly to the school there is no gift tax consideration and no limit on how much you may contribute? Talk to all those nice people who would have been willing to chip in toward the Coverdell ESA. Instead of limiting their combined contributions to $2,000, they could pay any amount at all directly to the school. True, there's no tax deduction for this. But they also won't have to file any gift tax returns, regardless of how much they contribute.

What is the value of this to the recipient? More than you can imagine. When families, religions, or communities require that their children attend private schools, the costs can be overwhelming. Even with scholarships to help out, there are still funds the parents must pay. In absolute dollar terms the additional costs might not seem high. But when you look at the supplement cost in terms of a percentage of the budget—especially if you must pay for more than one child—this can cause severe hardship.

Tip #204:

The consequence of not getting financial help when needed. When I came to California, my brother and I went to a small private religious school. Even with a financial hardship scholarship, our parents still had to pay $15 per month for each of us, or $30 per month. That doesn't seem like much, does it? After all, you spend more than that at Starbucks in a week, right? Uh huh.

Back then, that was 15 percent of our $200 mortgage. Today, that same house would rent for about $6,850 per month, or the mortgage would be about $5,900 per month. Without even taking cost-of-living inflation rates into account and just looking at the equivalent mortgage rates, that additional stipend would mean a copay of at least $885 per month, or $10,620 per year. It might explain why my father couldn't maintain those costs. Yes, he lost the house to foreclosure rather than asking for help from family members who might have been willing to pay our tuition shortfall. (If he had been able to keep the house, the mortgage would be long gone by now. The house would be worth more than $1.5 million! My brother is still fuming.) Let's not let that happen to you.

Tip #205:

Another way to save is the Qualified Tuition Program (QTP), also known as the Sec 529 plan (https://www.irs.gov/ publications/p970/ch08.html). Why is it called the Sec 529 plan (https://www.law.cornell.edu/uscode/text/26/529A)? Simple. That's the Internal Revenue Code section where you will find all the details. As with the other plans we have been discussing, there is no tax deduction for your contribution to the 529 plans. These plans were designed to allow family members to put a lot of money into a college savings plan. Essentially, the first year's contribution to the plan is designed to be quite large. Family and friends may contribute up to five times the annual gift tax limit, which is currently $14,000. Five times that amount is $70,000. When these plans became popular, I made up a detailed Benefit and Drawbacks list on the TaxMama.com site (http://taxmama .com/Articles/529.html).

Julie Garber, About.com's gift and estate planning guide, provides the updated annual gifting limits from 1997 to the current year (http://wills.about.com/od/understandingestatetaxes/a/ historygifttax.htm). This large initial contribution was valuable in several ways:

- Having a lot of money in the plan made it possible to invest in securities with higher returns than you could buy with lower balances.

- The big benefit of plans that were tied to specific educational institutions was that if you paid in a specified amount, your college tuition was guaranteed to be covered, regardless of the increase in fees over the years. (Of course, that guarantee was only valid at that institution or in that state. What if the student didn't want to attend that college, or wanted to study in a different state, when they grew up?)

- You could fund the account quickly for a student who would be starting college in just a few years.

- Some states may offer incentives that the IRS doesn't offer. They are well worth looking into.

- Funds could be used for tuition, books, and supplies as well as housing.

The drawbacks?

- Once that large initial deposit was made, the generous relative could make no more gifts to that person for five years.

- When you fill out the FAFSA (Free Application for Federal Student Aid) form for financial aid, the balance of the Sec 529 plan owned by you or your parents is taken into account (https://fafsa.ed.gov). *Note: If the trustee, who controls the plan, is a grandparent, you might not need to show the whole balance on your application.*

- Funds not used for educational purposes would face penalties when withdrawn from the account.

The details of these accounts have evolved a decade or two. Read the IRS overview in Publication 970 (https://www.irs.gov/publications/p970/ch08.html). Better yet, explore the excellent information on the Saving for College website (http://www.savingforcollege.com/college_savings_201). They can answer all your questions.

Tip #206:

Moving on from Sec 529 to Sec 529A. Young or old, sometimes you face disability issues. Have you ever heard of the ABLE Tax-Advantaged Accounts for Disabled Individuals (IRC Section 529A; https://www.law.cornell.edu/uscode/text/26/529A)? Most people have not because this is a new plan. You will find an excellent explanation by the good folks at www.smbiz.com. Let me give you a summary. Essentially this allows for contributions of up to $14,000 per year to go into a special bank account to help the person with a qualified disability. The "advantage" part of this account is that Medicaid and other aid programs won't take this bank account into consideration when they determine if the person is qualified for state aid. However, as with all tax benefits, there are drawbacks:

- The balance in the account can never exceed $100,000.

- Anything over that amount will be taken into account to reduce government aid and benefits.

- Excess annual contributions are subject to a 6 percent excise tax for each year until the excess amounts are removed.

- The funds may only be used for medical and support costs for the beneficiary.

- Any funds left in the account at death must be paid back to the various state aid programs up to the amount they contributed to the care of the individual.

Some benefits of the account include:

- There are no complicated legal processes to set up an ABLE account as there are in "special needs trusts" and the like.

- The funds may be used for funeral costs.

- You may pay legal and financial administration costs.

- The account balance may be transferred to another close relative who is disabled.

Bonus Tip #207:

News flash! The IRS just issued new rules to simplify how people can qualify for these accounts: https://www.irs.gov/pub/irs-drop/n-15-81.pdf. The guidelines were open to comment, and commenters noted that three of the requirements for qualified Achieving Better Life Experience (ABLE) programs in the proposed regulations would create significant barriers to the establishment of such programs. So the IRS simplified them. Please read the notice. These ABLE plans are brand new. States still need to establish guidelines, so check with the experts before trying to set these up on your own. Meanwhile, here are the changes:

- *Categorization of distributions not required.* ABLE programs need not include safeguards to determine which distributions are for qualified disability expenses, nor are they required to specifically identify those used for housing expenses. Commenters noted that such a requirement would be unduly burdensome and that, in any case, the eventual use of a distribution may not be known at the time it is made. Designated beneficiaries will still need to categorize distributions when determining their federal income tax obligations.

- *Contributors' TINs not required.* ABLE programs will not be required to request the taxpayer identification numbers (TINs) of contributors to the ABLE account at the time when the contributions are made if the program has a system in place to reject contributions that exceed the annual limits. However, if an excess contribution is deposited into a designated beneficiary's ABLE account, the program will need to request the contributor's TIN. For most people, the TIN is their Social Security number (SSN).

- *Disability diagnosis certification permitted.* Designated beneficiaries can open an ABLE account by certifying, under penalties of perjury, that they meet the qualification standards, including their receipt of a signed physician's diagnosis if necessary, and that they will retain that diagnosis and provide it to the program or the IRS upon request. This means that eligible individuals with disabilities will not need to provide the written diagnosis when opening the ABLE account, and ABLE programs will not need to receive, retain, or evaluate detailed medical records.

Watch for updates here: https://www.irs.gov/irb/2015-27_IRB/ar09.html. *Note: Section 303 of the PATH Act of 2015 changed the residency requirement for ABLE beneficiaries. Please see Bonus Tip #270 for more details.*

Tip #208:

Using whole life insurance to save up for college (or anything at all). This is something we haven't touched on at all. In early 2015, I was invited to do a TwitterChat for the @CollegePrepped team (http://collegeapptraining.com/chatcollege-on-tax-tips -and-preparation-for-parents-of-college-bound-students-recap). Via a link on their website I found a very thought-provoking article by Miguel Palma, CPA (http://www.mpalma.com/blog/life -insurance-better-bet-529-plan). I was wondering how he would make good on his statement "Why Life Insurance is a Better Bet than a 529 Plan." It's simple and brilliant, actually. You start funding the whole life policy for the child when the child is born or is very young. At that time, there are no health issues. The insurance companies are happy to take your money, knowing they will hold it for decades. The policy will build up value. When the child is ready to go to college, they simply borrow the funds. They can use the money for anything they choose without having to track the costs of books, fees, and so on. They won't have to care if the institution is accredited or not. There are no taxes on the borrowed funds. Either they can pay themselves back over the years or they can get a lower payout when they die or cash out the policy.

All right, since we started talking about education benefits anyway, let's move on to that topic!

CHAPTER 13

Tax Savings for Education

THE MOST VALUABLE THING in the world is a good education. It doesn't really matter what the education or major is, it's all about learning; learning how to think, how to research, knowing that you must ask questions and not take everything at face value. A free college education has even become a campaign issue. Will we get that here in the United States? Not anytime soon. But hopefully we will get ever more high-quality free colleges and universities, at least those operated by the cities and states.

For example, at present, the city college system in Southern California is expensive. A student carrying a full load (twelve to sixteen units) would pay about $550–$750 per semester at the Los Angeles City College or Pierce Community College, plus the costs of books, parking, and fuel or transportation. Add it all up and the cost for nine months' attendance, if the student lives at home, comes to a whopping $12,000 per year—more than $19,000 if they have to pay for housing (http://www.piercecollege .edu/pierce_fees.asp).

Clearly, we need some help. So where do we start? Let's look at tax benefits.

Tip #209:

Scholarships are great, but they are not always tax-free (https://www.irs.gov/taxtopics/tc421.html). You can use scholarship funds to cover the costs of tuition, fees, books, supplies, and mandatory course equipment. But if the scholarship covers more than that, like food, housing costs, travel, or optional equipment, you now have taxable income. This applies to grants, stipends, and even funds to Fulbright scholars. What's even worse is that if the scholarship is taxable, you will pay tax at kiddie tax rates—in other words, at your parents' highest tax rate.

Tip #210:

Tax-free education benefits at work. All employers can pay up to $5,250 of your education costs without the benefit being taxable to you. Anything over that and you pay tax on the benefit. It will be included in your wages (https://www.irs .gov/publications/p970/ch11.html). Is there a way around that? Maybe . . .

Tip #211:

Working benefit fringe. That's a nice little secret. When the education payments qualify as a working benefit fringe, none of the payments are taxable to you even if your employer pays out $30,000 or more. How do you get that? Well, it must be a written plan. The benefit must be available to all employees, without favoring "highly compensated employees," and it covers practically all costs except for tools and supplies that employees get to keep after the course ends. It cannot cover the owners of the business. But even small businesses can offer this benefit, say, to family members who don't meet the definition of "related parties" when it comes to ownership of the business. Read this information carefully and discuss it with the boss (https://www .irs.gov/publications/p15b/ar02.html). Incidentally, you cannot convert part of your wages to the education reimbursement. That would violate the provision that "the program does not allow employees to choose to receive cash or other benefits."

Tip #212:

Don't pay off your student loans, work them off instead. One of my all-time favorite television series was *Northern Exposure*. You have this clueless, newly graduated doctor, dropped into Alaska to perform, what to him, seemed like indentured servitude. Well, there really are federal and private programs that will pay off your student loans in exchange for a few years of your time (https://www.irs.gov/publications/p970/ch05.html). Now think about this and ask yourself these questions:

- How long will it take for you to pay off all your student loans? For many people, it could take ten to twenty years.

- During all that time, the loan is sitting on your credit, pushing down your FICO score. How do you feel about your credit?

- A big chunk of your wages goes toward the student loan payments, which means your standard of living is reduced—unless you spend like there's no tomorrow and just get deeper into debt. (This is dumb, but done.)

- Do you really need all that stress?

- How bad would it really be to go on an adventure for two or three years? Heck, you might even build up savings, meet the partner of your dreams, or at least learn more about life. And hey, think about all the great stories and pictures you will have!

Tip #213:

Let your student loans go into default. Yup. You might be able to give up and do that. Only it's not easy. Did you know that you cannot even bankrupt student loan debt? But let's say that you could somehow get the debt cancelled. Not only does that totally mess up your FICO score, it generates taxable income for cancellation of debt. So you are suddenly going to add $30,000, $50,000, or $200,000 to your income in the year you default on the loan. Talk about messing up your entire future. When you're having a tough time with the student loan, call the company, like a mensch, and work out more manageable payment arrangements.

Tip #214:

You're paying your student loan. Deduct the interest expense (https://www.irs.gov/publications/p970/ch04.html). You may deduct up to $2,500 of your interest payment. There are lots of strings on this deduction, including a limit to the amount of MAGI you may have before your deduction is reduced or eliminated (https://www.irs.gov/publications/p970/ch04.html). In fact, suppose you felt the interest rate was too high and you were able to refinance the loan at a better interest rate. You might have just changed the nature of the loan from a student loan to a personal loan. Interest on personal loans is not deductible at all. So be very careful—run the numbers. If you can get a low enough interest rate, you might be better off without any tax benefit at all.

- For instance, if you're paying 7 percent on a $60,000 loan, you're paying $4,200 in interest, right?

- Assuming you can save 30 percent (IRS and state tax rates) on $2,500 of that interest (or $750), your net interest expense out of pocket would be $3,450.

- Let's say you were able to refinance the loan to 4 percent. Your interest expense would be $2,400.

- Even without the interest deduction, you are more than $1,000 ahead.

Tip #215:

Now we come to the education deductions and credits. The nice thing about my professional tax software is that, for decades, I have been able to enter all the education and income data and tell the computer to select the best deduction or credit available to my clients. That doesn't mean the computer is always right. Sometimes I have to make some major adjustments and overrides to get the numbers to work because the computer isn't taking into account some key element. (Like last year, when my taxpayer's daughter ended up with a taxable scholarship and the software wasn't picking it up correctly.) Most of the time it works just fine. In recent years, the major consumer software houses like TurboTax, H&R Block, Computax, and TaxAct seem to have added this feature to their systems as well. If you are going to file your own tax return, make sure your tax preparation software offers you this benefit if you have education expenses.

Tip #216:

The tuition and fees deduction is worth $4,000 per tax return before it is reduced by your MAGI (https://www.irs.gov/publications/p970/ch06.html). I find that this deduction is often less useful than the two main tax credits. The main benefit of using the deduction instead of a credit is to reduce your AGI.

By bringing the Adjusted Gross Income down, you might free up a few more deductions on Schedule A, increase some other tax credits, or even reduce the impact of the Alternative Minimum Tax (AMT). I am not sure if tax software takes all these attributes into account all by itself. So if you find yourself generating AMT, or losing deductions or credits, see what happens if you use this deduction instead of an education credit.

Note: This has been extended through December 31, 2016, as Section 153 of the PATH Act of 2015. Please see Bonus Tip #270 for more details.

Tip #217:

The American Opportunity Credit (AOC) is worth up to $2,500 per eligible student on the tax return (https://www.irs.gov/publications/p970/ch02.html). The credit is computed as 100 percent of the first $2,000 of qualified education expenses, plus 25 percent of the next $2,000. You must be working on a degree to use this credit and in school at least as a half-time student for at least one full academic period during the current year—or the first three months of the following year. This is a favorite credit because it's partially refundable. That means even if you have no taxes due at all, you can still get back up to $1,000 per eligible student (or up to 40 percent of the total credit, if less than $2,500). This credit is only good for four tax years. They don't need to be consecutive years. As one IRS agent explained to me, plan out in advance which four tax years will give you the highest benefit for each student in the household. Oops. A student who has a felony drug conviction is not eligible for this credit. Good news: this credit was previously extended until December 31, 2017. Better news: this was made a permanent part of the Internal Revenue Code as Section 102 of the PATH Act of 2015. Please see Bonus Tip #270 for more details.

Tip #218:

The Lifetime Learning Credit (LLC) is worth up to $2,000 per tax return (https://www.irs.gov/publications/p970/ch03 .html). It is computed as 20 percent of the first $10,000 of qualified education expenses. No need to pursue a degree to claim this credit. All types of courses will qualify. No minimum number of courses is necessary, and no worries about felonies or drug convictions. Even former criminals are encouraged to learn. Although this credit is not available per student, one of the reasons it's worthwhile is this credit can be used to educate you in every year of your life. So if you're taking classes each year to improve your business skills, use this credit before taking deduction for employee business expenses. Whatever part of your education expenses you cannot use here, apply them toward your job if the courses are applicable.

Alas, it's a nonrefundable credit; if you have no tax liability, this credit is wasted. But good news: if one family member (spouse or dependent) qualifies for the AOC and another family member qualifies for the LLC, you may use them both on the same tax return—separately for each household member—up to the various limits.

Tip #219:

No double benefits are allowed for the same dollars spent. IRS Publication 970 repeats this concept over and over again, separately for each educational benefit (https://www.irs.gov/publications/ p970). In essence, the IRS walks you through the order in which tax attributes reduce the tuition. Before you may claim any expenses or credits, you must first reduce the tuition by scholarships and grants, draws from Coverdell ESAs and Sec 529 plans, refunds of the tuition, and other credits. Use Form 8863 for both these credits (https://www.irs.gov/pub/irs-pdf/f8863.pdf). Use a separate Part III (on page 2) for each student entitled to credits. To see how each credit is separately affected and limited, let's just pull the links directly from the index of Publication 970:

> American opportunity credit—No Double Benefit Allowed (https://www.irs.gov/publications/p970/ch02.html)
> Lifetime learning credit—No Double Benefit Allowed (https://www.irs.gov/publications/p970/ch03.html)
> Student loan interest deduction—No Double Benefit Allowed (https://www.irs.gov/publications/p970/ch04.html)
> Tuition and fees deduction—No Double Benefit Allowed (https://www.irs.gov/publications/p970/ch06.html)
> Work-related education—No Double Benefit Allowed (https://www.irs.gov/publications/p970/ch12.html)

Tip #220:

For the purpose of education, how do we adjust the Adjusted Gross Income (AGI) to arrive at the Modified Adjusted Gross Income (MAGI)? Here is an overview of the computation. It shows the items that are added back into income (mostly foreign income and housing exclusions) to arrive at the MAGI to be used for education deduction and credit purposes.

1. Enter the amount from Form 1040, line 22	1. _____
2. Enter the total from Form 1040, lines 23 through 33 ..... 2. _____	
3. Enter the total of any amounts entered on the dotted line next to Form 1040, line 36 ..... 3. _____	
4. Add lines 2 and 3	4. _____
5. Subtract line 4 from line 1	5. _____
6. Enter your foreign earned income exclusion and/or housing exclusion (Form 2555, line 45, or Form 2555-EZ, line 18)	6. _____
7. Enter your foreign housing deduction (Form 2555, line 50)	7. _____
8. Enter the amount of income from Puerto Rico you are excluding	8. _____
9. Enter the amount of income from American Samoa you are excluding (Form 4563, line 15)	9. _____
10. Add lines 5 through 9. This is your **modified adjusted gross income**	10. _____
Note. If the amount on line 10 is more than $80,000 ($160,000 if married filing jointly), you cannot take the deduction for tuition and fees.	

Tip #221:

We mention MAGI (Modified Adjusted Gross Income) in several places in this chapter (and elsewhere). However, please be aware that, thanks to the brilliant minds in Congress, MAGI has a completely different phaseout level of MAGI for each and every tax deduction, credit, and attribute.

- MAGI student loan interest—https://www.irs.gov/publications/p970/ch04.html

- Tuition and fees deduction MAGI—https://www.irs.gov/publications/p970/ch06.html

- American Opportunity Credit MAGI—https://www.irs.gov/publications/p970/ch02.html

- Lifetime Learning Credit MAGI—https://www.irs.gov/publications/p970/ch03.html

Table 4-2.Effect of MAGI on Student Loan Interest Deduction

IF your filing status is...	AND your MAGI is...	THEN your student loan interest deduction is...
single, head of household, or qualifying widow(er)	not more than $65,000	not affected by the phaseout.
	more than $65,000 but less than $80,000	reduced because of the phaseout.
	$80,000 or more	eliminated by the phaseout.
married filing joint return	not more than $130,000	not affected by the phaseout.
	more than $130,000 but less than $160,000	reduced because of the phaseout.
	$160,000 or more	eliminated by the phaseout.

Table 6-2.Effect of MAGI on Maximum Tuition and Fees Deduction

IF your filing status is...	AND your MAGI is...	THEN your maximum tuition and fees deduction is...
single, head of household, or qualifying widow(er)	not more than $65,000	$4,000.
	more than $65,000 but not more than $80,000	$2,000.
	more than $80,000	$0.
married filing joint return	not more than $130,000	$4,000.
	more than $130,000 but not more than $160,000	$2,000.
	more than $160,000	$0.

Limit on modified adjusted gross income (MAGI)	$180,000 if married filing jointly; $90,000 if single, head of household, or qualifying widow(er)

Limit on modified adjusted gross income (MAGI)	$128,000 if married filling jointly; $64,000 if single, head of household, or qualifying widow(er)

Tip #222:

Unreimbursed work-related education expenses. While you may not generally deduct the cost of a degree, if you can prove that specific expenses are job related, do claim them on your Form 2106 as employee business expenses. Read this Tax Court case, *Lori Singleton v. Commissioner*, from 2009 (http://www .ustaxcourt.gov/InOpHistoric/singleton-clarke.sum.WPD.pdf). It's quite interesting to read the story of this nurse who took a $14,787 deduction for the cost of her MBA/HCM (Health Care Administrator) on her 2005 tax return. She was able to prove that the new degree did not necessarily prepare her for a new job. It helped her maintain her skills for the job she already had. Singleton handled her own case and fought her own battle. She did a great job. That's why I am including her story. Generally, I would not have been so aggressive as to deduct the actual cost of the degree. But I would have taken the deduction for each individual course that helped a taxpayer maintain your skills for your present job or business. Keep your mind open to the possibilities (that are available within the law). And keep excellent records, as Singleton did.

Tip #223:

Need a summary? Due to the complexity and inconsistency of the laws related to the variety of tax credits and deductions related to education, it really helps to have a scorecard. Actually, in a way, the IRS does have such a thing. It's called Appendix B, "Highlights of Education Tax Benefits for Tax Year 20XX." This appendix is updated in each new year's edition of Publication 970. Alas, it's not available as we write this. But that doesn't mean you can't pull up the PDF version of this publication and click on Appendix B in the table of contents when you are working on your tax return (https://www.irs.gov/pub/irs-pdf/p970.pdf).

Really, seeing the overview of the various benefits, rules, and limits side by side will help you understand which ones you can use for yourself and your family.

Tip #224:

While we're talking about education, let's take a quick look at homeschooling to see if there are any tax benefits at all. For families who prefer to homeschool your children, consider getting a group of families together to share the responsibilities. If you can get state accreditation for the parents and for the school, it will be recognized as a school by the state. As a result, the IRS won't consider the teachers, principals, counselors, or aides to be homeschoolers. All accredited teachers may deduct their unreimbursed, class-related costs on line 23 (up to $250; see Tip #259) and the rest of the balance of costs on Form 2106 as itemized deductions. Remember, each "teacher" still has to meet the nine-hundred-hour test. For a ten-month teaching cycle, that's about twenty-one hours per week—or about three hours per day of a seven-day week. This wouldn't be easy to accomplish. A lot depends on why you are homeschooling. If it's to preserve security and your particular ideology, and you share it with others in the community, this may work for you.

CHAPTER 14

Tax No-No's

I HAVE NEVER BEEN ABLE to figure out why people make financial decisions based on what they hear from strangers in grocery lines, at bars, at Starbucks, or from what they see in cute pictures on Facebook, while ignoring their own financial advisors. This is especially true for really radical advice about ways to cut your taxes dramatically. Why aren't you getting your information from someone who can see your entire financial picture and give you advice based on your particular situation—not just on one piece of the picture or on urban myths?

Did you know that tax professionals around the country talk to each other? Yup. We are connected in closed groups on LinkedIn, Facebook, and other social media outlets where we share stories about your exploits. Of course, no one actually names any of our clients. We just tell our stories. Sometimes we laugh, sometimes we cry. Often we ask each other for advice.

The truth is, even though you come to us after you're in trouble, we really, truly want to help you.

That's exactly why I created TaxMama.com more than a decade ago. After having spent years as a troubleshooter for people with tax problems, I decided to try to help prevent the problems from ever happening in the first place by creating a free, safe place for you to ask your questions. You really, truly are welcome to come to TaxMama.com. Simply click on "Ask a Question." I, or another member of Team TaxMama, will give you an answer for free. (Please don't email us your questions—you won't get an answer. Period.) We won't compute your calculations or do the work for you. That would be impossible to do without a full-blown consultation, anyway. We will point you to the information you need. We will give you guidance on what to discuss with your tax professional. After all, if you don't know what to ask about or where to start in a consultation, it's a waste of time, isn't it?

OK, let's start the No-No's with the nightmare stuff. Have patience and work your way down to the routine things you never want to do.

Tip #225:

Don't play audit roulette. The odds are with the house (the IRS). It's really tempting to claim a large deduction for something that you didn't spend. Or to overvalue something that you sold so the profits are lower. Or to avoid reporting income that you got in cash or without a W-2 or 1099. After all, who's going to know? You're right. There are times you can get away with falsifying the information on your tax return—for a while. But the problem with this is that, as with winning when you gamble, it gets addictive. You get away with it once, looking over your shoulder all year . . . maybe for two years. No one comes after you. So let's try it again. The second time you do it and nothing happens, you're not quite as nervous. So you keep doing it. Sooner or later you will get caught. Yup. The IRS has better and better methods of cross-referencing information in your tax return with where you live, your lifestyle, your spending, and even your social media posts. The very deductions that you take tell the IRS when you are living above your reported means. Or, when you keep getting away with it, it's tempting to brag to a friend. Great friend. Uh huh. Your friend turns you in. People snitching on (former) friends, lovers, spouses, and neighbors are a big source of leads for the IRS. When the IRS does audit, and you have scammed them for several years, the IRS will start auditing previous years and give the information to your state(s).

Tip #226:

If you are going to play audit roulette, be smart. Keep your fake tax reductions to below 25 percent. That way, the IRS may only audit you for up to three years. (Your state may have an extra year or two, though.) When you underreport more than 25 percent of your income or tax liability, your exposure to audit is for at least six years. If the IRS can prove you were not just mistakenly underreporting but filing fraudulent tax returns, they may audit you as far back as they please. No limits. Not fun. This can even lead to criminal penalties and jail time.

Tip #227:

Don't fall prey to amateur tax geniuses. Friends who know everything and push tax advice on you will get you into trouble and you will end up coming to a tax professional quaking in terror. Why? The IRS is auditing that genius—and everyone with whom they shared their wisdom. You will end up paying a tax professional who will try to smooth over the truth and convince the IRS not to charge you penalties or bring criminal charges. There is nothing we can do about the taxes you will owe for doing something that was clearly not sensible. But the penalties and the interest on those penalties can run to the thousands of dollars. We can help prevent, reduce, or reverse those for you.

Tip #228:

Avoid the refund mills, those tax preparers in your community that have a reputation for generating really high refunds. How do you think that person is able to generate refunds that are so much higher than everyone else? Do they look smarter than your current tax professional? Do they even have a degree in accounting or taxation? Do they have an excellent reputation for integrity, known throughout the community as an expert? Heck no! Many of them are fly-by-night operators who will be long gone by the time the IRS comes to you asking for their money back. These kind folks not only rip the IRS off, they steal from you. Many of them give you one version of your tax return but file a different version. Their version has a higher refund. They have the part of the refund that you don't know about being deposited directly to their bank accounts. You will have to pay all that money to the IRS even though you didn't know it was happening.

Don't believe me? Think this is farfetched and TaxMama is exaggerating to scare you? Drop by the IRS's Criminal Investigation website. Click on the link to "Examples of Abusive Return Preparer Investigations" (https://www.irs.gov/uac/Abusive-Return-Preparer-Criminal-Investigation-%28CI%29).

Tip #229:

Speaking of penalties, don't waste your money getting saddled with tax penalties. Not only are they annoying and irritating, but you have to pay interest on the penalties. Practically all the time, if you are conscious of your responsibilities, you will have no reason to get a penalty. Of course, if you consort with tax wildcatters, watch out!

What are some of the regular penalties (https://www.irs
.gov/uac/Newsroom/Eight-Facts-on-Late-Filing-and-Late
-Payment-Penalties)?

- $135, or 100 percent of the unpaid tax if you file more than
  sixty days past the due date or extended due date of the return, whichever is lower.
- 10 percent for substantial understatement (§6662)
- 20–40 percent for accuracy-related penalties, specifically
  for gross under-valuations (§6662)
- 25 percent for delinquency (§6651)
- 25 percent, or 5 percent per month until you reach 25 percent, for late filing
- 25 percent, or ½ percent per month until you reach 25 percent, for late payment

What are the biggies?

- 75 percent for fraud (§6663)
- 75 percent for fraudulent failure to file (15 percent per
  month, up to 75 percent)
- $5,000 minimum for filing a frivolous tax return (§6702)

These are just the civil penalties. You don't even want to begin
to get involved with the criminal penalties.

Tip #230:

Don't pay IRS penalties. If you find yourself facing large IRS
penalties, get the penalties waived. Unless you're a tax criminal
or a habitual tax delinquent, there are often ways to get the IRS to
forgive penalties. For folks who've never gotten hit with penalties

before and suddenly face really large penalties, there is a special provision for you. It is called the First Time Penalty Abatement (FTA). You will find the details on the IRS website (https://www .irs.gov/Businesses/Small-Businesses-&-Self-Employed/Penalty -Relief-Due-to-First-Time-Penalty-Abatement-or-Other -Administrative-Waiver). Here are the three main qualifications to convince the IRS to waive your penalties:

1. You didn't previously have to file a return or you have no penalties for the three tax years prior to the tax year in which you received a penalty.

2. You filed all currently required returns or filed an extension of time to file.

3. You have paid, or arranged to pay, any tax due.

Tip #231:

If you owe a small penalty for something like not paying enough estimated taxes or withholding, just pay that penalty. Save the FTA for the big mistakes. Sometimes, with the complexity of the tax laws, even the most diligent Tax Vigilante will get hit.

Tip #232:

Don't disclose your Social Security Number (SSN) when not absolutely necessary. Naturally, you need to provide it to your employer, your medical care providers, and your bank. But really, unless you are in business, think twice, OK, three times, before giving it to anyone else. Do not have that number printed on your checks. And do not carry anything in your purse or wallet with your SSN. In my research for a MarketWatch.com article several years ago, I learned two disturbing sources of Social Security numbers theft:

1. SSNs were stolen when people applied for jobs.

   ○ Recommendation: don't give prospective employers your driver's license number or SSN until you are among the final candidates. And even then, make sure this is a legitimate employer, one that has been in the community for some time.

2. Baby's SSNs were stolen in the hospital. The hospital needs to file paperwork when the baby is born. The family would not be filing any tax returns for the baby or applying for credit for years, right? So someone in the hospital was selling the numbers. Parents would learn of this when opening savings accounts for their children.

   ○ Recommendation: get a family account, if possible, with your favorite credit bureau, preferably one of the big three—Equifax, Experian, Trans Union. Check the credit activity for each family member's SSN at least four times a year. Or simply freeze each child's credit until they need to use it. The bureaus even have information and tools related to child identity theft:

     ▪ Equifax—http://www.equifax.com/idtheftprotection kit (Disclosure: I have been writing a column for Equifax for several years: http://blog.equifax.com/author/eva-rosenberg)

     ▪ Experian—http://www.experian.com/data-breach/newsletters/child-identity-theft.html

     ▪ Trans Union—http://www.transunion.com/child identitytheft

Tip #233:

Don't become a victim of Stolen Identity Refund Fraud (SIRF). According to an August 2015 report, Treasury Inspector General for Tax Administration (TIGTA; https://www.treasury

.gov/tigta/auditreports/2015reports/201540026fr.pdf), approximately 1.1 million fraudulent tax returns were filed in 2011 that showed evidence of identity theft. Their words: "That have the same characteristics as IRS-confirmed identity theft tax returns." As a result, the IRS has started a campaign to make you aware of the issues, to solicit your help to stop this widespread fraud, and to help you become more active about protecting yourself. The campaign is called "Taxes. Security. Together." Get the details from the new IRS Publication 4524 (https://www .irs.gov/Individuals/Taxes-Security-Together). While most of the recommendations are common sense, it seems people are far too trusting and don't bother with precautions. Please don't think you are immune. You are not.

Tip #234:

Don't give out any information over the telephone to anyone who calls you about any identity, bank account, or tax or financial details. Even if (especially if) they seem to know a lot about you, do not answer or confirm their information. The best thing to do if the call is not from someone you actually know is to just hang up. If you feel that it might be a legitimate call, call the organization they claimed to be from and ask them if there are outstanding debts or medical or insurance issues. *Please, please, please, tell your parents and other elderly friends to hang up, as well. Help them avoid being victimized. Remember, you cannot be bullied if you hang up.*

For instance, even though I deal with the IRS all the time, if I am not expecting a call from them and someone calls me saying they are from the IRS, I won't discuss my client. I ask them their name, employee ID number, campus/location, and group number. I do get their phone number. Then I call the IRS directly. I do some research within my sources to determine if this person or phone number is legitimate. Hint: Google the phone number you were given to see if it is an IRS phone number. That saves time. If that doesn't work, you will need to call the IRS's main phone number, 1-800-829-1040. Tell the caller that you will call them back in a couple of days. If they tell you it's urgent and that you're about to be levied . . . beware. You would have gotten mail from the IRS if there were a levy notice. Another place you can call or visit is your local IRS office, where they have what's called Taxpayer Assistance Centers. Visit the IRS website and click on your state on this IRS map to get information (https://www.irs .gov/uac/Contact-Your-Local-IRS-Office-1).

Tip #235:

Never send money to anyone who calls you on the phone. If someone calls and tells you that you owe money to the IRS, the state, or on any outstanding bill, call that entity to ensure that you do owe the money and that the balance is correct. You can reach the IRS at 1-800-TAX-1040 (1-800-829-1040). Send your money directly to the IRS, state, or your creditor, not to someone who calls you and threatens you—especially if they want cash, money order, debit card, or cashiers' checks. First of all, the IRS doesn't make calls like that. Second, they never ask for cash, money order, debit card, or cashiers' checks. There are some very aggressive callers who may threaten you with po-lice action or even harm (https://www.irs.gov/uac/Newsroom/ Scam-Phone-Calls-Continue%3B-IRS-Identifies-Five-Easy -Ways-to-Spot-Suspicious-Calls). Truly, the easiest way to deal with them is to hang up. Many of my clients have gotten these calls but were smart enough to call me before sending money. I have at least one of these on my answering machine. Do not call them back and think you're going to play with them. If they are close enough to you to collect cash, they are close enough to do physical harm. If you do feel they are nearby and will harm you, call the police immediately.

People have actually given these scammers money. They have collected about $20 million according to TIGTA's recent estimate. The average amount people are bullied into giving them is $5,000. The highest payment reported is, believe it or not, *half a million dollars*!

Tip #236:

The last big scam: the IRS and the US Tax Code is unconstitutional. Puh-leeeze! If that were true, do you think anyone would still be paying taxes at all? Give me a break. Yet lots of smart people fall for the scam. The IRS has devoted an entire section of their website to help you understand the issues and why the "tax protester" movement is totally off base. The IRS puts these actions under the label of "Frivolous Arguments" (https://www .irs.gov/Tax-Professionals/The-Truth-About-Frivolous-Tax -Arguments-Introduction). This behavior earns criminal penalties, prosecution, and jail time (https://www.irs.gov/Tax-Professionals/ The-Truth-About-Frivolous-Tax-Arguments-Section-III).

I was once privileged to spend about three hours with the new IRS District Director in Los Angeles, Steven Jensen, interviewing him for an article in the *Los Angeles Daily News*. Our conversation ranged across many topics. This was one of them. I pointed out to him that these tax protesters generally cited specific Tax Code sections or sections in the US Code of Federal Regulations (CFR). Jensen asked if I had ever looked them up. The answer was no. So he proceeded to prove that their citations were generally meaningless. They made up cases and code sections to make their argument appear to have weight. But when you look them up, they are not even related to the point at all.

Even famous people fall for this. How many celebrities can you name? No, Richard Hatch of Survivor fame wasn't really a tax protester (http://www.newsmax.com/FastFeatures/

survivor-star-richard-hatch/2011/05/05/id/395272). He just didn't bother to pay taxes on more than $1 million worth of income.

Wesley Snipes did jail time (http://www.newsmax.com/ Hirsen/wesley-snipes-tax-evasion/2008/04/28/id/323538). Al Capone wasn't caught by "The Untouchables" but by the IRS and served jail time (https://www.irs.gov/uac/Historical-Documents -relating-to-Alphonse-%28Al%29-Capone,-Chicago). Joseph Andrew Stack III didn't do any jail time (http://www.newsmax .com/Headline/austin-attack-media-tea/2010/02/18/id/350266). Why? He slammed his airplane into an IRS building in Austin, Texas, and died.

Tip #237:

Don't assume the IRS will understand. TaxMama's other mantra: *disclose, disclose, disclose.* Whenever you have anything complicated or confusing in your tax return, explain it in detail. If you had to estimate something, include an explanation of why you don't have the actual amount and what source of information you used to come up with your estimate. If you needed to do a computation, include the detailed worksheet. Include information about account numbers and other specific information. When you provide details like this, it limits the IRS's audit powers to three years instead of six. Use the Form 8275 Disclosure Statement and add your attachments (https://www .irs.gov/pub/irs-access/f8275_accessible.pdf). If it turns out that you made some wrong assumptions, the full disclosure could eliminate penalties. If you relied on the advice of a tax professional, that surely will help eliminate penalties.

Good news: we are done with the nastiness. Let's get on with normal Tax No-No's!

Tip #238:

Whenever you have a Net Operating Loss (NOL), don't file your tax return without first deciding whether or not to waive NOL carryback (https://www.irs.gov/publications/ p536). This is a very common mistake, or oversight. Not making a decision about this can be extremely costly and could lead to audits. The average person doesn't realize this is necessary. In fact, in the rush to file on time, many tax professionals overlook this decision as well. It will be up to you to bring it up and ask about this if you see a negative AGI on your tax return. What the heck is TaxMama talking about? Good question.

The way the Internal Revenue Code is written, when you have a NOL (say in 2015), you are required to carry that loss back to your tax return two years earlier (to 2013). Once you use up that loss, you carry what's left to the tax return one year before the NOL year (to 2014). If there is still anything left, you carry it to the tax return for the year after the NOL year (to 2016). No doubt, our legislators thought that making this an automatic requirement would be helpful to taxpayers. But most people don't understand it and rarely use this provision. Because this requirement isn't understood, and because it is ignored, most people just take that loss and use it to reduce the next year's taxable income (2016). And *this* is what causes the audit. Since that's the wrong year, the IRS knows that when they audit they are guaranteed to generate additional taxes. So what's a good taxpayer to do? Let's look at the next tips, shall we?

Tip #239:

Don't carry the loss back. Waive your right to the carryback. If you could carry that loss back for two years and get refunds fairly quickly, why wouldn't you want to do it? Or why shouldn't you? Here are some reasons taxpayers may not want to file backward:

- As we discussed, most people just don't know about it, so they don't do it.

- Sometimes you have very little income in the earlier years and won't get enough of a tax reduction to make it worthwhile to file an amended return, so you would rather not bother.

- When you carry the loss back, you lose quite a bit of the loss because it gets eaten up by a variety of tax attributes. Besides, if your tax return for the carryback year shows losses, you get no benefit at all; you lose some or all of the value of the NOL by carrying it backwards.

- Some people have concerns over some tax issues in their returns in prior years. By filing an amended return, they open up that year's tax return to IRS scrutiny. They are afraid of an audit.

Tip #240:

Don't forget to include the "election statement" in your tax return in the year the NOL is created. What statement? The statement must be attached to your timely filed tax return, including extensions. It must read something like this: "I am choosing to waive the carryback period for tax year 20XX under section 172(b)(3)." This tells the IRS that you will be using the loss in future years only.

Your tax software has this built in for you to use. You just have to know where to find it. If you cannot find the checkbox for it, call tech support and ask them. Otherwise, file your tax return on paper and include that election. Feel free to use my wording.

Tip #241:

Oops, you forgot to make the election, or didn't know. Can you still fix it? No worries . . . uh, well, no worries if it is less than six months since you filed the tax return. Here's what you do. The IRS explains it beautifully: "If you filed your original return on time but did not file the statement with it, you can make this choice on an amended return filed within six months of the due date of the return (excluding extensions). Attach a statement to your amended return and write, 'Filed pursuant to section 301.9100-2' at the top of the statement" (https://www .irs.gov/publications/p536/ar02.html).

Tip #242:

Supposing you do want to use the carryback, don't forget to file Form 1045 before the end of the year. Most people, when they think about filing an amended personal tax return, think about Form 1040X. But when it comes to NOLs, there is a special form, Form 1045, Application for Tentative Refund (https:// www.irs.gov/pub/irs-access/f1045_accessible.pdf). This form is special for several reasons:

- It is primarily designed to use when you have a NOL.

- It lets you include amendments for several years on one form. (This is especially important in certain years when we are able to carry losses back for up to five years.)

- It is meant to generate a refund more quickly than if you had filed the Form 1040X—instead of having to wait for four months or more, this should be faster—but only if you attached absolutely everything to explain your NOL and your adjustments to the prior years.

- It must be filed by December 31 of the year in which you file the tax return that generated the NOL. For instance, suppose you file the 2015 tax return by October 15, 2016. You must use the Form 1045 by December 31, 2016. If you miss the deadline, no worries. You simply have to file the separate Form 1040X for each carryback year.

Tip #243:

Don't deduct costs related to pets, no matter how strongly you feel that they are part of your family. The IRS doesn't accept them as dependents. Yet. Huh? Why *yet*? Believe it or not, in 2009, Representative Thaddeus McCotter, who represented a Detroit-area district, introduced the HAPPY (Humanity and Pets Partnered through the Years) Act (http://www.newsmax .com/InsideCover/mccotter-pets-taxes/2009/08/25/id/334603). It was designed to authorize a deduction of up to $3,500 a year for "qualified pet care expenses," including veterinary care. Of course, it was not successful. But expect more of this thinking as the population ages.

Tip #244:

Don't overlook allowable deduction for service pets. Seeing eye dogs, hearing dogs, and other service pets' costs are fully deductible as medical expenses. Naturally, you need a prescription from your doctor. The pet must be specially trained to help you with your particular medical need. You can find more information about service animals at Assistance Dogs International (http://www.assistancedogsinternational.org/about-us/ types-of-assistance-dogs/service-dog). They are overseen by the Americans with Disabilities Act (ADA). You can find their FAQs on the ADA site (http://www.ada.gov/archive/animal.htm).

Tip #245:

Don't deduct your swimming pool or hot tub energy costs when applying for the Residential Energy Credit on Form 5695. The rules say, "Costs allocable to a swimming pool, hot tub, or any other energy storage medium which has a function other than the function of such storage do not qualify for the residential energy efficiency credit" (https://www.irs.gov/pub/irs-pdf/i5695.pdf).

Tip #246:

Don't deduct the cost of over the counter drugs or certain non-Western medicines. They are not deductible in Flexible Spending Accounts, Health Savings Arrangements, or itemized deductions on Schedule A. Nowhere. People argue and try. However, there is one exception: when the over-the-counter drugs are prescribed by a doctor (in writing) for the treatment of a specific condition. Certain non-Western or nontraditional medical practitioners are recognized by the IRS. You will find them in IRS Publication 502 (https://www.irs.gov/publications/p502). Keep a copy of the prescription. Get a new copy every year. Have the doctor's office write a letter, each year, explaining why these over-the-counter drugs are prescribed instead of behind-the-counter drugs. Here are the IRS's FAQs about this issue (https://www.irs.gov/uac/Affordable-Care-Act:-Questions-and-Answers-on-Over-the-Counter-Medicines-and-Drugs). Regardless of other limitations, insulin is always deductible, whether purchased over or behind the counter.

Here are some nondeductible drugs, even with prescriptions: laetrile, medical marijuana, and other drugs bought outside the US that are not approved by the FDA. Incidentally, in the latest budget bill, Congress quietly stopped all prosecution for businesses selling medical marijuana in states where that is legal.

Tip #247:

You may not deduct the cost of cosmetic surgery if the surgery is for purely personal reasons (https://www.irs.gov/publications/p502/ar02.html). However, if there is a medical reason for the cost, you may claim the deduction. What is the best way to prove there is a medical reason? If your health insurance company provides all or partial reimbursement, there's a good chance there is a medical reason for the procedure. Still, it's a good idea to get a copy of the prescription or doctor's paperwork showing the medical need for the surgery. Common acceptable reasons include reconstructive surgery after an accident (a fire), an earlier surgery (like breast removal), or a birth defect (cleft palate). Sometimes the medical reason might be psychological—severe depression, perhaps even threatening suicide, because of a visible defect.

Tip #248:

Don't withdraw money from your 401(k) or other retirement plan to pay for education, your first house, or other exclusions. You may have heard that there are a few expenses that are exempt from the early withdrawal penalty, but that only applies if the money is drawn from an IRA—not from any other retirement account (see Tip #194).

Tip #249:

Never deduct commuting mileage (https://www.irs.gov/publications/p463/ch04.html). This is the mileage from home to your office or your job, a trip you take regularly. (I found this out, early in my career, the hard way. During an audit. It was embarrassing, but we had a good laugh.) However, if you drive from home to an alternate work location, or to class, or training, and so on, that is not commuting. You may also track the mileages from the office to those other locations, or to a second job. This rule applies equally to people with jobs and business.

Tip #250:

Paying off a loan is not a deduction, no matter how big that loan is. A long time ago I had an angry discussion with a client who was also my roommate. She had borrowed about $50,000 to buy Nautilus® equipment for her gym. We took a depreciation deduction for all that equipment either in the first year, or over the first five years, that she was in operation. One day, a new boyfriend came along and paid off her loan. He insisted that she must get a deduction for that payment. Despite explaining patiently three or four times, and even providing detailed worksheets about how the numbers worked, he didn't believe me. They stalked out of my office in fury. I haven't heard from them since. Over the years, I have had similar discussions with other clients. All the rest understood the concept after a while. I hope you do, too. If there are deductions to be had, the deductions were used when the loan was first obtained and the assets were purchased. If it was a business loan, the interest was deducted each year as the payments were made. But the payoff? No deduction. The journal entry on the books would be:

Debit—Loan Balance (a liability)
Credit—Cash (the bank account)

Tip #251:

You may not claim a deduction for the cost of fees relating to loan modification documents and or IRA transfers. When it comes to loan modifications, if the loan is on a home, you might be able to add it and the other costs to the basis (tax cost) of the home. There is no deduction at all for fees related to student loans and other loans. For investment loans, you may take a deduction under Miscellaneous Itemized Deductions and reduce the cost by 2 percent of your Adjusted Gross Income.

Tip #252:

Don't claim a deduction for the annual IRA fees or transfer fees unless you paid the fees with money outside the account. Most people let the fees come from the funds inside the IRA. That means you are reducing your investment each year. It's wiser to pay the costs with money out of your pocket. The fees are relatively low. If you are able to use Miscellaneous Deductions, you will be able to deduct the fees. If not, your IRA will grow just that little bit more.

Tip #253:

Don't let the IRS audit you year after year. It's actually their own rule about "Repeat Examinations." If a return was examined for the same items in either of the two previous years and no change was proposed to the tax liability, contact the IRS immediately and the examination will likely be discontinued. This policy is in accordance with section 7605(b) of the Internal Revenue Code, which states that no taxpayer shall be subjected to "unnecessary examinations" (https://www.law.cornell.edu/uscode/text/26/7605). So what do you do if they invite you back to the dance again? If it's for the same issues—and the IRS found nothing the first time—just call them up and politely explain that they need to cancel the audit. Please, do be polite. Being rude, arrogant, and pushy will only get you into trouble. After all, Martha Stewart didn't go to jail because of a small amount of insider trading profits. She went to jail because was rude to the investigators and brushed them off. They had power. They used it. Had she cooperated, most likely she would have simply been embarrassed, slapped on the wrist, and fined.

Tip #254:

Do not rely on the IRS instructions, written or verbal. There is an excellent article by attorney Robert W. Wood on Forbes.com (http://www.forbes.com/sites/robertwood/2015/11/11/amazingly -irs-says-you-cant-rely-on-irs-instructions). Wood provides a long list of taxpayers who relied on the IRS's instructions and lost in court. If you're going to take a position on a tax issue that you think is a little borderline or aggressive, get a written opinion from an Enrolled Agent, Certified Public Accountant, or an attorney. That will give you standing. The IRS's public information will not.

Tip #255:

Don't leave your tax refunds on the table. You only have three years to file a tax return after the end of the tax year. If you don't file . . . whoosh! The money is gone. Every year, the IRS posts its announcement about unclaimed refunds (https://www.irs .gov/uac/Does-the-IRS-Have-Money-Waiting-For-You%3F). Millions of dollars go unclaimed. In 2015, the IRS announced that there was about $1 *billion* sitting there, waiting for you. Sure, it's nice to make a large donation to the coffers of the US Treasury. But . . . you don't even get a donation deduction for this. And do you really want your government officials just wasting your tax refund? Heck no! File on time and waste that money yourself.

Tip #256:

Don't leave assets unclaimed. Visit the unclaimed property sites in the states where you or your family have ever lived. Start at the USA.gov (https://www.usa.gov/unclaimed-money) site to look up your states—that way you know that you are dealing the real states' websites, not someplace bogus. (Warning: If someone calls you or sends you an email saying they have found assets for you, do not give them any money or information. If they refuse to provide you with details, visit the unclaimed property sites yourself. There is a lot of fraud out there.) You would be surprised what family members may have left behind in bank accounts, insurance policies, wages, security deposits, and so on. After the entities lose touch with the account owners, they are required to turn the assets or money over to the state. I found several thousand dollars that belonged to my deceased aunt.

Tip #257:

Never fall for a "too good to be true" tax preparer or investment offer. If it looks too good to be true, it probably is. Sure, you like to believe in Santa Claus, Peter Pan, and fairy tales. The fantasy world is a delightful escape and I go there often. But when you enter that world, please leave your money and your tax returns behind.

CHAPTER 15

Adjusting or Itemizing—What's the Difference?

W E ALL KNOW THAT people try to increase their tax deductions as much as possible to reduce their total tax hit. The truth is tax deductions are actually quite troublesome and have a whole raft of disadvantages and limits. What's wrong with itemized deductions (which are reported on Schedule A)?

- You already have a substantial standard deduction (2016) for Single & Married Filing Separately $6,300, Head of Household $9,300, or Married Filing Jointly & Qualifying Widow(er) $12,600. (You can find the most recent standard deduction numbers at the Tax Policy Center: http://www.taxpolicycenter.org/taxfacts/displayafact.cfm ?DocID=171&Topic2id=30&Topic3id=34.)

- In order to get any benefit from your itemized deductions, they must be higher than the standard deduction associated with your filing status. This means you lose the benefit of the automatic deduction provided by the IRS in the first place.

- Most of your deductions have limits or reductions. For instance:

  ○ Medical deductions are reduced by 10 percent of your AGI (or only 7.5 percent if you or your spouse are still under age 65 through December 31, 2016).

  ○ If you deduct the state income taxes that you paid, you may have to pay taxes on any state income tax refunds the following year (see Tip #42).

  ○ Miscellaneous Itemized Deductions are reduced by 2 percent of your AGI.

  ○ Investment interest deductions are limited to your investment income. And if you use the investment interest deduction, it might cost you the special capital gains rates on some, or all, of your capital gains and dividends.

  ○ Mortgage interest deductions are limited on several levels:

    ▪ You may only deduct the interest on the original mortgage on the home, increased by loans for repairs and remodeling *plus* up to $100,000 of additional home equity debt.

    ▪ If you refinance the mortgage, you may only deduct the interest on the balance of that original mortgage plus that $100,000 mentioned above. So if you took cash out . . . you might not be able to deduct the mortgage at all.

    ▪ If you are rich and have a very high original mortgage, you may only deduct the interest on the first

$1,000,000, plus that additional $100,000 of home equity debt. You'd be surprised at how many people get caught in this trap.

• Itemized deductions are further limited by a phaseout. Your deductions are reduced as your income rises above $258,250 or more ($309,900 for married couples filing jointly). This is adjusted for inflation each year.

• To make matters even worse, your itemized deductions are apt to be reduced by the Alternative Minimum Tax (AMT).

• Last but not least, with high itemized deductions, you increase your chances for audit.

So you can see why you actually want to avoid those deductions, if possible, and aim for adjustments to income instead of itemized deductions. That way you can keep the full benefit of those standard deductions and reduce your audit risk. For 2015 updates, phaseouts, and so on, see https://www.irs.gov/uac/News room/In-2015-Various-Tax-Benefits-Increase-Due-to-Inflation -Adjustments.

Tip #258:

Adjustments are the Form 1040's best kept secret. Let me show you something that most people working on their own taxes often overlook. These are the "above the line" deductions called Adjustments to Income. The "line" is the bottom line on page 1 of the Form 1040—usually, line 37. Line 37 is also generally referred to as your AGI.

| 37 | Subtract line 36 from line 22. This is your **adjusted gross income** . . . . . ▶ | 37 | | |

23	Educator expenses	**23**			
24	Certain business expenses of reservists, performing artists, and fee-basis government officials. Attach Form 2106 or 2106-EZ	**24**			
25	Health savings account deduction. Attach Form 8889 .	**25**			
26	Moving expenses. Attach Form 3903	**26**			
27	Deductible part of self-employment tax. Attach Schedule SE .	**27**			
28	Self-employed SEP, SIMPLE, and qualified plans . .	**28**			
29	Self-employed health insurance deduction	**29**			
30	Penalty on early withdrawal of savings	**30**			
31a	Alimony paid **b** Recipient's SSN ▶	**31a**			
32	IRA deduction	**32**			
33	Student loan interest deduction	**33**			
34	Tuition and fees. Attach Form 8917	**34**			
35	Domestic production activities deduction. Attach Form 8903	**35**			
36	Add lines 23 through 35				**36**

Tip #259:

There appear to be 13 deductions you can use above the line. Although this is the usual list, in the past two of these deductions had to be renewed by Congress each year—the $250 educator deduction (line 23)and the $4,000 tuition and fees deduction (line 34). Just as we went to press, Congress passed the PATH Act of 2015. The $250 educator deduction has been made a permanent part of the Internal Revenue Code, as Section 102 of the PATH Act of 2015. And the $4,000 tuition and fees deduction has been extended to December 31, 2016, as Section 153 of the PATH Act of 2015. Please see Bonus Tip #270 for more details.

Tip #260:

Line 36, Total Adjustments. Shhh . . . don't tell anyone. More secrets for you. Although the Form 1040 shows 13 items you may deduct "above the line," line 36 lets you use another 9 adjustments. Who knows—some of them might just apply to you. After the next tip, we will discuss the key adjustments that might affect your financial life. Meanwhile, here's the information about the hidden adjustments straight out of the IRS instructions to the Form 1040, for line 36 (https://www.irs.gov/pub/irs-dft/f1040-dft.pdf):

- Archer MSA deduction (see Form 8853). Identify as "MSA."
- Jury duty pay if you gave the pay to your employer because your employer paid your salary while you served on the jury. Identify as "Jury Pay."
- Deductible expenses related to income reported on line 21 from the rental of personal property engaged in for profit. Identify as "PPR."
- Reforestation amortization and expenses (see Pub. 535). Identify as "RFST."
- Repayment of supplemental unemployment benefits under the Trade Act of 1974 (see Pub. 525). Identify as "Sub-Pay TRA."
- Contributions to section 501(c)(18)(D) pension plans (see Pub. 525). Identify as "501(c)(18)(D)."
- Contributions by certain chaplains to section 403(b) plans (see Pub. 517). Identify as "403(b)."
- Attorney fees and court costs for actions involving certain unlawful discrimination claims, but only to the extent of gross income from such actions (see Pub. 525). Identify as "UDC."
- Attorney fees and court costs you paid in connection with an award from the IRS for information you provided that helped the IRS detect tax law violations, up to the amount of the award includible in your gross income. Identify as "WBF."

Table V. **Other Adjustments to Income**

Use this table to find information about other adjustments to income not covered in this part of the publication.

IF you are looking for more information about the deduction for...	THEN see...
Certain business expenses of reservists, performing artists, and fee-basis officials	Chapter 26.
Contributions to a health savings account	Publication 969, Health Savings Accounts and Other Tax-Favored Health Plans.
Moving expenses	Publication 521, Moving Expenses.
Part of your self-employment tax	Chapter 22.
Self-employed health insurance	Chapter 21.
Payments to self-employed SEP, SIMPLE, and qualified plans	Publication 560, Retirement Plans for Small Business (SEP, SIMPLE, and Qualified Plans).
Penalty on the early withdrawal of savings	Chapter 7.
Contributions to an Archer MSA	Publication 969, Health Savings Accounts and Other Tax-Favored Health Plans.
Reforestation amortization or expense	Chapters 7 and 8 of Publication 535, Business Expenses.
Contributions to Internal Revenue Code section 501(c)(18)(D) pension plans	Publication 525, Taxable and Nontaxable Income.
Expenses from the rental of personal property	Chapter 12.
Certain required repayments of supplemental unemployment benefits (sub-pay)	Chapter 12.
Foreign housing costs	Chapter 4 of Publication 54, Tax Guide for U.S. Citizens and Resident Aliens Abroad.
Jury duty pay given to your employer	Chapter 12.
Contributions by certain chaplains to Internal Revenue Code section 403(b) plans	Publication 517, Social Security and Other Information for Members of the Clergy and Religious Workers.
Attorney fees and certain costs for actions involving certain unlawful discrimination claims or awards to whistleblowers	Publication 525.
Domestic production activities deduction	Form 8903, Domestic Production Activities Deduction.

Tip #261:

In IRS Publication 17 on Table V, the IRS provides a list of the main adjustments to income, linked to the places where you can find more details. The table (http://www.irs.gov/pub/irs-pdf/p17.pdf) also includes some of the adjustments we mentioned in the previous tip. We discuss the adjustments in the various chapters about education, investment, retirement, and so on. *Note: We won't be covering any of the business deductions (lines 27–29 and line 35) though—that's a whole other book. I just wanted you to be aware that you can use these special deductions.*

Tip #262:

Jury pay. When you do jury duty, always make sure to ask for mileage reimbursements at the outset. If your court system

allows for mileage compensation, generally the only time to secure that is at the very beginning. When you are paid for your
jury duty by the court, you will get a 1099 from them even
though the compensation is often quite minor. Some employers are kind enough to pay you while you are off on jury duty.
They usually require you to turn over the jury pay to them as a
token repayment. If your company has you do that, deduct that
amount on line 36 and write "Jury Pay."

Tip #263:

PPR. Deductible expenses related to income reported on line 21
from the rental of personal property engaged in for profit. This
requires a bit of translation. "Personal property" is anything you
rent out that is not real estate or a vehicle (there are other places
to report those rentals). What are some examples? You work in
the film industry and get a rental fee for your camera. You are a
set designer and keep a supply of all kinds of furniture, accessories, fabrics, and other unique items you have collected over the
years, so you get a "kit fee." You work in construction and have
a special set of your own tools or equipment. What do you rent
to your employer?

You report the rental income for your personal property on
line 21 of the Form 1040 as Other Income. You can deduct any
costs related to the personal property rental here. Such costs
might include depreciation, repairs, refurbishment of the asset,
cleaning fees, and storage fees. Keep a good record of the costs
and related receipts in your tax return file for the year. Deduct
those amounts on line 36 and write "PPR."

Tip #264:

UDC. Attorney fees and court costs for actions involving certain unlawful discrimination claims, but only to the extent of

gross income from such actions. Generally, attorney fees are only deductible as itemized deductions. You can't even imagine the unfairness of this! Because of this requirement in the Tax Code, some people who win judgments end up owing more in taxes than they netted after paying legal fees, administrative costs, and medical costs. However, when it comes to unlawful discrimination, you are allowed to deduct the legal fees here, above the line, up to the amount of your gross income from the settlement. What is "unlawful discrimination?" It includes all these types of discrimination: age discrimination, sex discrimination, and employment discrimination.

If you received such a judgment and paid attorney fees, consider reading the IRS's "Lawsuits, Awards, and Settlements Audit Techniques Guide": https://www.irs.gov/pub/irs-utl/lawsuites awardssettlements.pdf.

Tip #265:

WBF. Attorney fees and court costs you paid in connection with an award from the IRS for information you provided that helped the IRS detect tax law violations, up to the amount of the award includible in your gross income. This is the "whistleblower reward." If you turn someone in (see the following tip) and the IRS ends up paying you, you are allowed the privilege of deducting your attorney fees and costs above the line. If turning someone in also costs you jail time, it's not clear if you are permitted to include those attorney fees here. You may want to pay a good tax professional to research that for you. Why? Is it even possible for you to get an award but still go to jail? You bet! Read on.

Tip #266:

Did you know that you can get a substantial reward for turning in someone you know is cheating on their taxes? Yep. In fact, there is a special form for that, Form 211, Application for Award for Original Information (https://www.irs.gov/pub/irs -pdf/f211.pdf). Bradley Birkenfeld earned about $104 million for turning in his employer, UBS, in 2008 (http://www.marketwatch .com/story/irs-whistle-blowing-for-fun-and-profit-2012-09-19). (Probably the biggest award ever.) The IRS was able to examine the finances of major tax evaders who stashed their funds in secret Swiss accounts and collected a fortune in back taxes, penalties, and interest. Birkenfeld was paid a percentage of the amount the IRS collected. But . . . he went to jail for his own participation in the bank fraud. He's done his time and feels great about the $104 million he received from the IRS (http://www .newsmax.com/Newsfront/ubs-whistleblower-birkenfeld-arrest/ 2015/11/08/id/701199). How does this affect you? If you know of someone who is cheating on their taxes to the tune of a couple of million dollars or more, you can report them to the IRS using that Form 211. When you do, be sure you can tell the IRS where their assets can be found. After all, if the IRS cannot collect on the judgment, you cannot get paid. If the IRS decides to investigate and is able to locate the tax evader's funds, you will get a percentage of the recovery. Naturally, that award is taxable—report it on line 21 as "Other Income." Sometimes a tax evader is violent and vengeful. In that case, consider remaining anonymous. Use an experienced IRS whistleblower attorney to represent you. Apparently, Birkenfeld's attorneys did not do a good job protecting him or he would not have landed in jail. Regardless, many people do get these judgments. If you do, and you have attorney fees and court costs, deduct them on line 26 and write "WBF."

Tip #267:

Medicare. One extra adjustment not mentioned in the IRS publication is legal fees paid for a private cause of action under

Medicare Secondary Payer statute (http://www.teaguecampbell
.com/private-cause-action-medicare-secondary-payer-act).
What does this mean? Sometimes when someone is injured or
ill they turn to Medicare to pay their medical expenses. Suppose
they have workers compensation, other insurance coverage,
or employer coverage, and Medicare determines that one (or
more) of those coverages should reimburse Medicare. If Medicare does not get reimbursed, they will file a conditional reimbursement lien and collect from the taxpayer. The taxpayer can
then sue their various other providers. When they win and get
a settlement, that settlement will be taxable. You are permitted
to deduct these legal fees above the line. Since the IRS doesn't
provide a code, consider using "Medicare." Be sure to include
an explanation with details. File this tax return on paper, not
electronically.

Tip #268:

The other obscure stuff for line 36. If any of those things apply
to you, do consider sitting down with a tax professional who is
an expert in those areas. They are not generally common issues
in self-prepared returns.

Tip #269:

**Repayments under a Claim of Right for repayments of more
than $3,000**. This isn't really an adjustment. It can be an item-
ized deduction or, best of all, it can be a tax credit. What does
this mean? Well, let's start with the easy part. "Repayments" are
anything you have to repay on which you paid tax. This could
be unemployment income, if they found out you were actually
working; wages or sign-on bonuses repaid to an employer; excess Social Security income because your earned income was
too high; and so on. You would think that since you paid tax on

this income in a prior year, you should simply be able to deduct the reimbursement on line 21 as negative "Other Income," right? If only that were the case. Alas, no. When the repayments are under $3,000, you are forced to deduct the amounts as Miscellaneous Itemized Deductions on Schedule A. These deductions are reduced by 2 percent of your AGI, like most Miscellaneous Itemized Deductions. You get no benefit from these deductions if you can't itemize. When the reimbursement is more than $3,000, you get to take a tax credit instead of a deduction (or you may use the deduction, but not have it reduced by 2 percent of your AGI). Tax credits are better than deductions. They reduce your taxes, dollar for dollar.

OK, here's the complicated part. To get that tax credit, you need to go back to the tax return for the year when you originally reported this income. Deduct the amount you are paying back and recompute the tax return. Print it out. The difference between your original total tax liability and your reduced income is the tax credit you will use. IRS Publication 525 has some examples of how this computation works—look for "Repayments" in the index (https://www.irs.gov/publications/p525/ix01.html). If you must reimburse funds that cover several tax years, you might have to do several years' worth of recomputations and claim the credit in the year in which you pay back all the money. (No, you would not amend those earlier years.) If the credit is significant, do file your tax return on paper and include copies of all the revised prior-year tax returns, each marked "COPY." Incidentally, sometimes the deduction works better than the credit. Compute the repayment both ways. Better yet, get a tax pro who understands this claim or right to help you. (Warning: Very few tax pros know about this credit option.)

Bonus Tip #270:

On December 18, 2015, Congress passed sweeping legisla-
tion in the form of this bill—"Protecting Americans from
Tax Hikes Act Of 2015 (or PATH)." This bill makes some
tax provisions permanent, so taxpayers will not have to wait
in suspense, until the end of every year. Here is a link to the
House Ways and Means Committee's summary of the key provisions of the proposed PATH Act: http://waysandmeans.house
.gov/wp-content/uploads/2015/12/SECTION-BY-SECTION
-SUMMARY-OF-THE-PROPOSED-PATH-ACT.pdf

A Few Last Words

I LOVE WRITING FOR YOU and helping guide you through the treacherous shoals of the US tax system's surging seas.

I love researching tax issues from a different perspective. Sometimes I even take on challenges like the one that got me my MarketWatch.com column at Dow Jones. In the Introduction, I promised to tell you the story.

In 2002, I started getting emails from a TaxMama.com subscriber named Roger B. Adams. He was an American tax preparer in Portugal. Wow . . . that was impressive. He sent me this one email about a situation where a client had made an investment of about $700,000 into a company—and lost it all due to the president's mismanagement or theft. If his client reported this as a capital loss, they would only be able to deduct $3,000 per year in excess of any capital gains. Since this client had lost his money, there were no capital gains anticipated in the foreseeable future. In other words, it would take more than two hundred years to deduct these losses.

Adams's question was whether there was enough justification to claim this as a casualty loss. Doing that would let them deduct the full amount in the year of the loss. Since there would obviously be a lot of loss left over, it would become a Net Operating Loss (NOL; see Tip #251). They could carry the loss back two years and forward for fifteen years (see Tip #255). This client would get immediate refunds and not owe taxes for a decade or so. This way, at least, Adams's client would be able to recoup some of his money.

Hmmm . . . I read the question and thought, oh you poor naïve, inexperienced tax professional. I proceeded to spend twenty minutes writing up an explanation of what casualty losses really are and why this isn't a casualty loss. Feeling very smug, I was about to press the send button when a light went off over my head. (Yeah, exactly like in a cartoon.)

Wow! He's a genius! What if this is a theft loss. If he can prove the president of the company deliberately defrauded the client, this strategy would work. Of course, he would have to file a police report—and they would probably have to get the attorney general to file charges. But with this much money at stake . . . it was worth pursuing.

I got really excited. Erased everything I had written and wrote a whole new enthusiastic response. Roger (no longer Mr. Adams) and I spent a lot of time researching this. Meanwhile, Roger sat for and passed the IRS's Special Enrollment Examination and became an Enrolled Agent. Now he had status—he was no longer just some tax pro out in some foreign country. (In fact, he is now the only tax professional listed on the IRS website for Certified Acceptance Agents in Portugal [https://www.irs.gov/Individuals/Acceptance-Agents---Portugal].)

I asked every expert at the IRS that I knew of to please look over our logic and tell us if this was reasonable. They all warned me this made no sense and we would get into trouble taking this position.

But Roger and I believed the IRS was wrong. So I had him write an article about this. Admittedly, his first draft was rather stiff and pedantic, but I knew I could punch it up. So I started calling publications that I was already writing for to see if they would be interested in his article. No one was interested in this article by some guy they had never heard of. Then one of my editors referred me to Chris Pummer at MarketWatch.com. He was polite but firm. Absolutely not.

But wait! Plummer went on to say, "One of my columnists just got a new gig and can't file his article for this week. If you can get me an article within an hour, the rest of the column (six more weeks) is yours." After swooning from joy, I recovered quickly and got him the article within about an hour and a half. (It took us a half hour to determine the best topic.) The rest is history. Because I tried to help a reader (who became a special friend), I have now been writing for MarketWatch.com (and sometimes for the *Wall Street Journal*) for more than a dozen years. (See, sometimes, good deeds do get rewarded!)

Oh yes, whatever happened to the notorious article about the casualty theft loss? We got my rewrite of it published in time for Valentine's Day 2004 (http://www.marketwatch.com/ story/when-might-stock-losses-count-as-a-theft-claim). Roger got credit for the information. I turned my fee over to him. He has been teaching International Tax Law at TaxMama's EA Exam School for years (http://irsexams.com/instructors/#roger).

And the IRS? Uh oh. The IRS had a fit! They were so upset with me that they issued Notice 2004-27 warning taxpayers that they could not use this casualty loss treatment for stocks purchased on the open market even if the officers had been convicted of criminal offenses (https://www.irs.gov/irb/2004-16_IRB/ar09.html).

Ironically, in one of the last paragraphs of the notice, they inadvertently pointed out that Roger's and my treatment was kosher:

In cases involving stock purchased on the open market, the courts have consistently disallowed theft loss deductions relating to a decline in the value of the stock that was attributable to corporate officers misrepresenting the financial condition of the corporation, even when the officers were indicted for securities fraud or other criminal violations. In *Paine v. Commissioner*, 63 T.C. 736, *aff'd without published opinion*, 523 F.2d 1053 (5th Cir. 1975), the taxpayers claimed a theft loss deduction for a decline in value of stock stemming from misrepresentations of the financial status of the corporation by corporate officials. ***The court noted that the taxpayers did not purchase the stock from the corporate officers who made the misrepresentations, but on the open market.***

Since, in fact, the situation was all about buying the stock directly from the corporate officer, this IRS notice specified that the casualty loss treatment was valid.

In fact, this same treatment was the foundation of the IRS's position on how to treat the Bernie Madoff and other Ponzi scheme losses (https://www.irs.gov/uac/Commissioner-Shulman's-Senate-Finance-Testimony-on-Ponzi-Schemes-and-Offshore-Tax-Evasion-Legislation).

The point to all this? Don't rely on the IRS's interpretation of the tax laws passed by Congress. After all, the courts don't. If you firmly and honestly believe you are right—do the research (or pay someone with experience to do the research).

The US Internal Revenue Code is a fluid and growing body of law. It's actually rather fun to swim in this sea! And remember, if you have good tax tips or stories, please send them to me at DeductEverything@gmail.com. If your stories are included in the next book, you will receive a TaxNerd T-Shirt with your name on it. You may pick the three S's—*style, sex, and size*—or even select one for your baby (http://www.zazzle.com/taxnerd+clothing).

Glossary

THIS IS NOT INTENDED to be a comprehensive set of definitions of all tax terms—just some of the main words, acronyms, and concepts in this book that TaxMama thinks need a bit more clarification. Some of the definitions include additional tax tips. Consider them a bonus.

For a more complete set of definitions, you can find a terrific glossary on the IRS's VITA training site (https://apps.irs.gov/app/understandingTaxes/student/glossary.jsp). And yes, VITA is defined in the following entries.

Adjusted Gross Income (AGI)—the number on the very last line of your Form 1040 page 1. It is also the same number on the first line of your Form 1040 page 2. This number is only found and clearly visible on the long form, not the

Form 1040 EZ or 1040-A. You will see this acronym used throughout this book. This number is very important. It is the basis for all IRS income limits, phaseouts of credits and deductions, reductions of itemized deductions, and more. It affects the Alternative Minimum Tax, your tax bracket, and practically every tax benefit and loophole there is. So if you remember nothing else, please remember the AGI.

Americans with Disabilities Act (ADA)—rules from the ADA affect medical deductions and related credits.

Beneficiary—the person who gets the "benefit" from any number of things. It could be from an IRA, pension plan, estate, insurance policy, or a gift. It's a good idea to review all your policies and accounts to make sure that you are showing the correct beneficiary. (For instance, my husband still shows his father as the beneficiary of one of his pensions. Pop died in 2007.) It's important to remove former spouses or other people who are no longer in your life. If you have minor children, do not name them as beneficiaries. Name a trust to be created on their behalf as the beneficiary to avoid court oversight on every single expenditure.

Code of Federal Regulations (CFR)—the entire body of US law. You can find the most current version on the Government Publishing Office's website (http://www.gpo.gov/fdsys/browse/collectionCfr.action?collectionCode=CFR).

Covenants, Conditions, and Restrictions (CC&Rs)—these rules bind all owners of condominiums, co-ops, and some communities or cities. These are the rules that define noise levels, outside parking, the color(s) you may paint the exterior of your home, how frequently you must mow your lawn, and if you are permitted to put up holiday decorations. Before buying a home in any community, the seller is required to give you a copy. Most people don't read them. You should. Once you do, you may find that you don't want to live in a community with some of the restrictions included in the CC&Rs. Finding out after you buy the home can be a disaster and make you hate your new home or community.

Dividend Reinvestment Programs (DRIPs)—this is when you buy stock and use the company's dividends to buy more of their stock. Generally, you have no fees, or the fees are very low (see Tip #198).

Earned Income—to the IRS, this means the total of all your wages and your self-employment profits. Self-employment profits can be found on your Schedule C and your general partnership income, which is passed through to you from a Form 1065 via a Schedule K-1. This income is reported on the Schedule E, page 2. (Schedule E, page 1 is generally passive income only.) Sometimes you have miscellaneous income that is considered self-employment as well. That would be found on line 21 of your Form 1040. To determine your total earned income easily, add up your wages and line 3 of your Schedule SE, Self-Employment Tax (https://www.irs.gov/pub/irs-pdf/f1040sse.pdf). Why is earned income important? This is the basis for a variety of credits as well as the limit for all IRA and retirement contributions.

First Time Penalty Abatement (FTA)—this is a special provision of Tax Code that allows people to get large penalties waived by the IRS. You may only use this provision once (as in "first time"). You must meet some rigorous qualifications, including never having gotten into tax trouble before and being in compliance now. There are other procedures to help you get other kinds of penalties cancelled.

Frequently Asked Questions (FAQs)—the IRS has many pages with FAQs on a variety of subjects. Some of the pages are helpful. Some, not as helpful. However, if you find that some of their information is seriously unclear, or lacking in usefulness, do me a favor. Send me the link to the page and tell me what you feel is missing. Tax-Mama will ask the IRS to update it. And believe me, the IRS is pretty responsive to those requests. When I can give them specific wording or specific suggestions, they make the changes in days rather than months. Send your notes to DeductEverything@gmail.com.

In Compliance—when the IRS talks about being "in compliance," they mean this:

- You have filed all the tax returns you are required to file—personal, business and payroll.

- You have paid all your taxes through withholding or via estimated tax payments.

- For people who owe a great deal of money and want special dispensations, it means you have paid all *this year's* taxes through withholding or via estimated tax payments.

Individual Retirement Account (IRA)—this is exactly what it says: an IRA is for a distinct individual. Couples do not share IRAs. Each person has their own. (I explain because this is a common misconception.) However, you will generally specify your spouse or child as your beneficiary. IRAs come in several flavors—plain, Roth, deductible, nondeductible. So it's important to track your IRA contributions and accounts.

Internal Revenue Code (IRC)—also known as Title 26 of the US Code of Federal Regulations (see CFR). You can find the most current version on the Cornell University Law

School's website (https://www.law.cornell.edu/uscode/
text/26). Please donate money to them if you use it regularly. I do.

LITCs—(see VITA)

Modified Adjusted Gross Income (MAGI)—for certain tax
benefits or attributes, the IRS modifies the AGI by adding things like nontaxable income to it or removes certain taxable items to create a different threshold. Because
the IRS uses different revisions to AGI for different deductions and credits to arrive at MAGI, this is generally
confusing and inconsistent. When reading anything that
refers to a MAGI, you need to look up exactly what the
modifications are and what income ranges apply.

Net Operating Loss (NOL)—this amount is generated from business losses or business or personal casualty losses. While
ending up with any losses is always a bad thing, the consolation is that when it comes to NOLs, you can deduct the full
amount in the year of the loss and carry the unused losses to
earlier years or future years, whichever work better for you.

Preparer Tax Identification Number (PTIN)—by law, each
paid preparer must put this on your tax return in the signature area of your tax return. If it's missing from a paid
tax return, report the preparer to the Internal Revenue
Service   (https://www.irs.gov/Tax-Professionals/Make-a
-Complaint-About-a-Tax-Return-Preparer). They are operating illegally. If they say they didn't know they should
have used a PTIN, that means they are so totally out of
touch with the current Tax Code that you should avoid
them like the plague. Any tax return they prepare will be
wrong or falsified.

Qualified Education Expenses (QEE)—this can mean different things depending on the education tax benefit you want to use. In all cases, tuition, fees, books, and course supplies are included. However, in some cases, transportation and housing are also included. Before using any education tax or credit, it's important to look up the conditions tied to that tax benefit.

Refund—this is a return of your money from the IRS or state. It could also be a payment to you from refundable credits that you may have earned. Many people call this a "return," which is incorrect.

Refundable Credits—credits from which you can get money back without paying anything in. They are often targets of tax scammers and identity thieves. Refundable credits change from year to year, depending on Congress' whim. However, they consistently include these credits:

- Additional Child Tax Credit
- American Opportunity Credit
- Earned Income Credit
- Health Coverage Tax Credit
- Credit for Prior Year Minimum Tax

Required Minimum Distributions (RMDs)—this is the minimum amount required to be withdrawn from a senior's taxable retirement accounts once they turn age 70½. They may always draw more money, but not taking the minimum draws can subject them to huge penalties (see Tip #166).

Return—a tax return or form. It does not mean a refund. So when you use the word *return* to refer to your tax refund and you see bewildered looks on the face of your tax professional, it's because it takes us a while to understand what you're talking about.

Tax Basis—the tax value of your asset(s) (https://www.irs.gov/taxtopics/tc703.html). Sometimes it's what you paid for it, plus the cost of improvements. Other times it's what the person who gave it to you paid for it, plus their cost of improvements. When you inherit the asset, it could be the fair market value on the date of death or six months after death. It's a lot more complicated than it appears to be. In fact, in college, they can spend weeks teaching the concept. Why is this so important? Because in order to know how much your profit is when you sell something, you must know the basis of the asset being sold. When someone bought an asset a long time ago and doesn't have records, this could make a huge difference. A perfect example of this is Walmart stock. If you had invested $5,000 in 1970, that stock would have been worth about $65 million by 2011 (http://askville.amazon.com/todays-original-share-walmart-stock/AnswerViewer.do?requestId=83432494). That same $5,000 invested in 1980 would have only been worth $26 million by 2011. (This is very raw and approximate data from an unknown source. But it illustrates the concept.)

Tax Clinic—(see VITA)

Tax Liability—this is not the balance due on the bottom of your tax return. It is the total amount of your taxes for the year after deducting all your credits but before deducting your payments. You used to be able to find that number on line 63 of the long Form 1040, where it now says "Total Tax." However, if you look below that, you see several refundable tax credits that reduce the total tax. So the form no longer shows you the tax liability. You must do the math yourself. Still remember how to subtract?

Taxpayer Identification Number (TIN)—any number used by a taxpayer. For American individuals, this would be their

Social Security Number (SSN). For foreigners, it would be an Individual Taxpayer Identification Number (ITIN). An adopted foreign child would get an Adoption Taxpayer Identification Number (ATIN) until their SSN was issued. For businesses, this would be an Employer Identification Number (EIN). There are a variety of other specialized numbers issued to tax professionals for a variety of purposes. The one that's important for you to see on every tax return prepared by a tax professional that you pay is the PTIN.

TCE—(see VITA)

Social Security Administration (SSA)—you know these folks. This is the agency that runs the Social Security system. They have a useful website: https://www.ssa.gov/.

Stolen Identity Refund Fraud (SIRF)—trying to stop this type of fraud is a major goal for the IRS and all divisions of the US Treasury. They claim that more than $30 billion has been stolen via identity theft fraud (http://www.justice.gov/tax/stolen-identity-refund-fraud). If we could stop this, do you think Congress would cut our taxes?

Volunteer Income Tax Assistance Program (VITA)—this system also includes the Tax Counseling for the Elderly (TCE), which is often run by the American Association for Retired Persons (AARP; https://www.irs.gov/Individuals/Free-Tax-Return-Preparation-for-You-by-Volunteers). They also include the Tax Clinics, also known as the Low Income Taxpayer Clinics (LITC; https://www.irs.gov/Advocate/Low-Income-Taxpayer-Clinics), which are often run by colleges or universities with student volunteers. There are sites all over the country. They all provide free services to taxpayers who need them. The primary targets are people whose incomes fall below specified amounts and seniors.

Resources

YOU WILL FIND UPDATES and notes about this book on our special website: www.deducteverythingbook.com.

Get free answers to your tax questions from Team TaxMama. Visit TaxMama.com and click on "Ask a Question." *Note: This is the* only *place to get free answers from TaxMama. Please do not send emails expecting answers.*

This section contains links that are elsewhere in the book, organized in a semi-logical fashion. It also contains links to resources that are favorites of TaxMama that you will enjoy using.

Oh yes, if you want TaxNerd gear or TaxMama swag, here are the places to go. You can even customize everything with your name, URL, or company name: http://www.zazzle.com/taxmama. Drop by www.TaxNerd.net if you don't want to bother with customization and if you want lots more variety. (Besides, it's an easier URL to remember.)

Disclosure: A few of the links might provide a commission to TaxMama. (Most do not.) But that's not why they are here. She would recommend them without a commission. Incidentally, at some of the places TaxMama recommends, if you tell them Tax-Mama sent you, you might get a discount. Call them before you buy anything.

Before we get started, a bit of irony, or *Catch-22*ism. Here is the *Forbes* article by Robert W. Wood, "Amazingly, IRS Says You Can't Rely on IRS Instructions": http://www.forbes.com/sites/robertwood/2015/11/11/amazingly-irs-says-you-cant-rely-on-irs-instructions.

Note: All URLs are subject to change. If you find errors, please let us know and we will post the changes at www.deductevery thingbook.com.

Record-Keeping Resources

The Bean Counter site is adorable—http://www.dwmbean counter.com
The Bookkeeping Master—https://www.youtube.com/watch?v=IhYJbCAcCKE
Mint—https://www.mint.com
Outright—http://outright.com
QuickBooks—http://quickbooks.intuit.com
Quicken—http://www.quicken.com/stay-connected-your-money
Shoeboxed—http://www.shoeboxed.com

Good, Old-Fashioned Paper-Based Systems

Accordion Files—http://www.staples.com/Staples-Accordion-Letha-Tone-Expanding-Files/product_SS119099

Dome Record Books—http://www.domeproductsonline.com/
dome-books

SafeGuard One-Write Systems—https://www.gosafeguard
.com/business-checks/one-write-systems

Tax MiniMiser—http://taxminimiser.com

Wilson Jones Accounting Supplies—http://www.wilsonjones
.com/wj/us/us/s/2252/accounting-suppliesaspx

Record-Keeping Apps

DeductR—https://app.deductr.com/taxmama

Expensify—https://www.expensify.com

FreshBooks—https://taxmama.freshbooks.com/signup

ItsDeductible by Intuit—https://turbotax.intuit.com/
personal-taxes/itsdeductible

MetroMile's mileage app—https://www.metromile.com/
technology

Finding a Good Tax Professional

AARP Tax-Aide—http://www.aarp.org/money/taxes/aarp
_taxaide or call 888-687-227

Filing complaints about tax professionals—http://www.irs
.gov/Tax-Professionals/Make-a-Complaint-About-a-Tax
-Return-Preparer

Find Certified Public Accountants (CPAs)—http://www
.aicpa.org/FORTHEPUBLIC/FINDACPA/Pages/
FindACPA.aspx

Find Enrolled Agents (EAs)—National Association of Enrolled Agents—http://www.naea.org

Find a Tax Attorney—American Bar Association Tax Section—
http://www.americanbar.org/groups/taxation.html

IRS database of PTIN-holders with some sort of tax
education—http://irs.treasury.gov/rpo/rpo.jsf
LITC—Low Income Taxpayer Clinics—http://www.taxpayer
advocate.irs.gov/about/litc
VITA & TCE—free help from IRS volunteer sites—https://
www.irs.gov/Individuals/Free-Tax-Return-Preparation
-for-You-by-Volunteers

Prepare Your Own Tax Return

Complete Tax—http://www.completetax.com/index.html
Drake's 1040.com—https://www.1040.com
Free-File Alliance members the IRS—http://freefilealliance
.org/free-file-alliance-members
Free-File options from the IRS—http://www.irs.gov/uac/Free
-File%3A-Do-Your-Federal-Taxes-for-Free
H&R Block—http://www.hrblock.com
TaxAct—https://www.taxact.com
TaxSlayer—https://www.taxslayer.com/compare-tax-software
TurboTax—https://turbotax.intuit.com

Prior-Year Software

Free Tax USA (I don't know them, but they look interesting)—
http://www.freetaxusa.com/prior_year.jsp
TaxAct—https://www.taxact.com/products/all_previous.asp
Also, check your favorite tax software to see if they offer
prior-year software, now that the IRS is accepting electronic filing for two to three prior years.

IRS Forms Mentioned in This Book

Form 211—Application for Award for Original Information (Application for Whistleblower Reward)—https://www .irs.gov/pub/irs-pdf/f211.pdf

Form 1023—Application for Recognition of Exemption Under Section 501(c)(3) of the Internal Revenue Code— https://www.irs.gov/pub/irs-pdf/f1023.pdf

Form 1040—https://www.irs.gov/pub/irs-pdf/f1040.pdf

    Form 1040 Schedule C—Profit or Loss from Business— https://www.irs.gov/pub/irs-pdf/f1040sc.pdf

    Form 1040 Schedule E—Supplemental Income and Loss—https://www.irs.gov/pub/irs-pdf/f1040se.pdf

    Form 1040 Schedule H—Household Employment Tax— https://www.irs.gov/pub/irs-pdf/f1040sh.pdf

    Form 1040 Schedule SE—Self-Employment Tax—https:// www.irs.gov/pub/irs-pdf/f1040sse.pdf

Form 1045—Application for Tentative Refund (for NOL carrybacks) https://www.irs.gov/pub/irs-access/f1045 _accessible.pdf

Form 1098-C—Contributions of Motor Vehicles, Boats, and Airplanes—https://www.irs.gov/pub/irs-pdf/f1098c.pdf

Form 1099-K—Payment Card and Third Party Network Transactions—https://www.irs.gov/pub/irs-pdf/f1099k.pdf

Form 1099-MISC—Miscellaneous Income—https://www .irs.gov/pub/irs-pdf/f1099msc.pdf

Form 2120—Multiple Support Declaration—https://www .irs.gov/pub/irs-pdf/f2120.pdf

Form 3903—Moving Expenses—https://www.irs.gov/pub/ irs-pdf/f3903.pdf

Form 5329—Additional Taxes on Qualified Plans (Including IRAs) and Other Tax-Favored Accounts—https://www .irs.gov/pub/irs-pdf/f5329.pdf

Form 5498-SA—HSA, Archer MSA, or Medicare Advantage MSA Information—https://www.irs.gov/pub/irs-pdf/f5498sa.pdf

Form 5695—Residential Energy Credits—https://www.irs.gov/pub/irs-pdf/f5695.pdf

Form 6251—Alternative Minimum Tax—https://www.irs.gov/pub/irs-pdf/f6251.pdf

Form 8275—Disclosure Statement—https://www.irs.gov/pub/irs-access/f8275_accessible.pdf

Form 8283—Noncash Charitable Contributions—https://www.irs.gov/pub/irs-pdf/f8283.pdf

Form 8606—Nondeductible IRAs—https://www.irs.gov/pub/irs-prior/f8606-2015.pdf

Form 8826—Disabled Access Credit—https://www.irs.gov/pub/irs-pdf/f8826.pdf

Form 8829—Office in Home—https://www.irs.gov/pub/irs-pdf/f8829.pdf

Form 8863—Education Credits—https://www.irs.gov/pub/irs-pdf/f8863.pdf

Form 8889—Health Savings Accounts (HSAs)—https://www.irs.gov/pub/irs-access/f8889_accessible.pdf

Form 14039—Identity Theft Affidavit—https://www.irs.gov/pub/irs-pdf/f14039.pdf

Form W-7—Application for IRS Individual Taxpayer Identification Number—https://www.irs.gov/pub/irs-pdf/fw7.pdf

Form W-9—Request for Taxpayer Identification—https://www.irs.gov/pub/irs-pdf/fw9.pdf

IRS Publications and the Tax Code Mentioned in This Book

The best Internal Revenue Code online—at Cornell University—https://www.law.cornell.edu/cfr/text/26/chapter-I (remember to donate once in a while)

IRS Regulations—Code of Federal Regulations—http://www.gpo.gov/fdsys/browse/collectionCfr.action?collectionCode=CFR

IRS Publication 17—Your Income Tax (the master of all IRS publications for individuals)—http://www.irs.gov/publications/p17

IRS Publication 463—Travel, Entertainment, Gift, and Car Expenses—https://www.irs.gov/publications/p463

IRS Publication 502—Medical and Dental Expenses—https://www.irs.gov/publications/p502

IRS Publication 521—Moving Expenses—https://www.irs.gov/publications/p521

IRS Publication 525—Taxable and Nontaxable Income—https://www.irs.gov/publications/p525

IRS Publication 526—Charitable Contributions—https://www.irs.gov/publications/p526

IRS Publication 527—Residential Rental Property—https://www.irs.gov/publications/p527

IRS Publication 536—Net Operating Losses (NOLs) for Individuals, Estates, and Trusts—https://www.irs.gov/publications/p536

IRS Publication 561—Determining the Value of Donated Property—https://www.irs.gov/publications/p561

IRS Publication 915—Social Security and Equivalent Railroad Retirement Benefits—https://www.irs.gov/publications/p915

IRS Publication 925—Passive Activity and At-Risk Rules—https://www.irs.gov/publications/p925

IRS Publication 936—Home Mortgage Interest
Deduction—https://www.irs.gov/publications/p936

IRS Publication 946—Depreciation—https://www.irs.gov/
publications/p946

IRS Publication 969—Health Savings Accounts and Other
Tax-Favored Health Plans—https://www.irs.gov/
publications/p969

IRS Publication 970—Tax Benefits for Education—https://
www.irs.gov/publications/p970

IRS Publication 4524—Security Awareness for Taxpayers—
https://www.irs.gov/pub/irs-pdf/p4524.pdf

IRS Publication 5027—Identity Theft Information for
Taxpayers—https://www.irs.gov/pub/irs-pdf/p5027.pdf

IRS Resources

Certified Acceptance Agents—Locate someone, anywhere
in the world, who is certified to help aliens get their
ITINs without having to send original documents to
the IRS (never to be seen again)—https://www.irs.gov/
Individuals/Acceptance-Agent-Program

Find your local IRS office—https://www.irs.gov/uac/
Contact-Your-Local-IRS-Office-1

Get an IRS ID Number for Aliens—the
ITIN—the Individual Tax Identification
Number—https://www.irs.gov/Individuals/
Individual-Taxpayer-Identification-Number-ITIN

Glossary from the IRA VITA training site—https://apps.irs
.gov/app/understandingTaxes/student/glossary.jsp

Health Care Marketplace Tips from the IRS—http://content
.govdelivery.com/accounts/USIRS/bulletins/1246e5b

Identity Theft Resources—https://www.irs.gov/Individuals/
Identity-Protection

Internal Revenue Manual—https://www.irs.gov/irm

IRS Criminal Investigation website, in all its glory!—https://
www.irs.gov/uac/Abusive-Return-Preparer-Criminal
-Investigation-%28CI%29

IRS FIRE—Filing Information Returns Electronically—
https://www.irs.gov/Tax-Professionals/
e-File-Providers-%26-PartnersFiling-Information
-Returns-Electronically-%28FIRE%29

IRS First-Time Penalty Abatement or Other Administrative
Waiver—https://www.irs.gov/Businesses/Small-
Businesses-&-Self-Employed/Penalty-Relief-Due-to-First
-Time-Penalty-Abatement-or-Other-Administrative
-Waiver

IRS Foreign Currency Rates—https://www.irs.gov/
Individuals/International-Taxpayers/Yearly-Average
-Currency-Exchange-Rates

IRS Lawsuits, Awards, and Settlements Audit Techniques
Guide—https://www.irs.gov/pub/irs-utl/lawsuitesawards
settlements.pdf

IRS Penalties—https://www.irs.gov/uac/Newsroom/Eight
-Facts-on-Late-Filing-and-Late-Payment-Penalties

IRS Standard Mileage Rates—http://www.irs.gov/
Tax-Professionals/Standard-Mileage-Rates

IRS Warning to Avoid Tax Refund Products—http://www
.irs.gov/uac/Tax-Refund-Related-Products

The Truth about Frivolous Arguments (a.k.a. Tax
Protesters)—https://www.irs.gov/Tax-Professionals/
The-Truth-About-Frivolous-Tax-Arguments-Introduction

IRS Charity Resources

Applying to set up an Exempt Organization or Charity—
https://www.irs.gov/Charities-&-Non-Profits/
Applying-for-Tax-Exempt-Status
IRS Charitable Donations from IRAs—https://www.irs.gov/
Retirement-Plans/Charitable-Donations-from-IRAs
IRS Charity Look-Ups—https://www.irs.gov/Charities
-&-Non-Profits/Exempt-Organizations-Select-Check
IRS Tax Information for Charities and Other Non-Profits—
https://www.irs.gov/Charities-&-Non-Profits
Life Cycle of an Exempt Organization—https://www.irs
.gov/Charities-&-Non-Profits/Life-Cycle-of-an-Exempt
-Organization

Other Charity-Related Resources

Crazy Cat Lady Takes on the IRS—http://taxmama.com/
tax-quips/crazy-cat-lady-takes-on-irs
The Foundation Center—great place to look up exempt
organization data and tax reports without having to log
in—http://foundationcenter.org/findfunders/990finder
GrantSpace—lots of information and resources about tools
to help nonprofit organizations—http://grantspace
.org/tools/knowledge-base/Funding-Research/
Forms-990-and-990-PF/finding-990-990-pfs
GuideStar—the original site with information about
charities—must log in to get free information. Some
reports require payment—http://www.guidestar.org/
Home.aspx
Shelters for Israel—a group started by housewives that
disburses close to 100 percent of their revenue for

charitable purposes—http://www.sheltersforisrael.com/about-us

TechSoup—http://www.techsoup.org

Volunteering Opportunities—What's the point of sitting alone in your room? Come out to the world and play!—https://www.volunteermatch.org

IRS Retirement, Education, and Savings Resources

ABLE new simplified guidance from the IRS—https://www.irs.gov/pub/irs-drop/n-15-81.pdf

ABLE Tax-Advantaged Accounts for Disabled Individuals (IRC Section 529A)—https://www.law.cornell.edu/uscode/text/26/529A

Coverdell Education Savings Accounts (ESAs)—https://www.irs.gov/publications/p970/ch07.html

Employer-Provided Educational Assistance—https://www.irs.gov/publications/p970/ch11.html

FAFSA—Free Application for Federal Student Aid—https://fafsa.ed.gov

IRA Contribution Limits—https://www.irs.gov/Retirement-Plans/Plan-Participant,-Employee/Retirement-Topics-IRA-Contribution-Limits

IRA Deduction Limits—https://www.irs.gov/Retirement-Plans/IRA-Deduction-Limits

IRA One Rollover per Year Rule—https://www.irs.gov/Retirement-Plans/IRA-One-Rollover-Per-Year-Rule

Qualified Tuition Program (Sec 529 Plan)—https://www.irs.gov/publications/p970/ch08.html

Required Minimum Distributions from all Retirement Plans—https://www.irs.gov/Retirement-Plans/Plan-Participant

,-Employee/Retirement-Topics-Required-Minimum
-Distributions-%28RMDs%29
Roth IRAs—https://www.irs.gov/Retirement-Plans/Roth
-IRAs
Scholarships and Grants Information—https://www.irs.gov/
taxtopics/tc421.html
Sect 72t Election—Drawing Retirement Funds in Substan-
tially Equal Periodic Payments—https://www.irs
.gov/Retirement-Plans/Retirement-Plans-FAQs
-regarding-Substantially-Equal-Periodic-Payments
Tax Theft Loss Notice 2004-27—https://www.irs.gov/irb/
2004-16_IRB/ar09.html
Tax Theft Loss and Ponzi Schemes, a-la-Bernie Madoff—
https://www.irs.gov/uac/Commissioner-Shulman's
-Senate-Finance-Testimony-on-Ponzi-Schemes-and
-Offshore-Tax-Evasion-Legislation

Taxpayer Advocate Resources and TIGTA

Reports to Congress—http://www.irs.gov/Advocate/
Reports-to-Congress
The Taxpayer Advocate Service—Headed by Nina E. Olson.
Call her team when you really need help and the IRS is
ignoring you—https://www.irs.gov/Advocate
TIGTA—Treasury Inspector General for Tax Administra-
tion—J. Russell George, the man heading the team that
audits the IRS—https://www.treasury.gov/tigta

Social Security Resources

Social Security—Minimum Annual Earnings to Qualify for Benefits—https://www.socialsecurity.gov/oact/cola/QC.html

Social Security Benefit Calculation Example—https://www.ssa.gov/oact/progdata/retirebenefit1.html

Social Security Disability Planner website—https://www.socialsecurity.gov/planners/disability/dwork2.html

Social Security website—https://www.socialsecurity.gov

State Resources and Other Government Resources

All state tax agencies—http://www.taxadmin.org/state-tax-agencies

All state tax forms—http://www.taxadmin.org/state-tax-forms

American with Disabilities—http://www.ada.gov

California Film Commission—http://www.film.ca.gov/How_to_Market.htm

California Probate Referees—http://www.sco.ca.gov/eo_probate_contact.html

California Publication 1005—Pension and Annuity Guidelines—https://www.ftb.ca.gov/forms/2013/13_1005.pdf

Energy.gov—Energy Credit Resources—http://energy.gov/savings

EnergyStar—https://www.energystar.gov

PACE—http://energy.gov/eere/slsc/property-assessed-clean-energy-programs

Scientific American—on Iceland's use of geothermal power—http://www.scientificamerican.com/article/iceland-geothermal-power

New York City Mayor's Office—Filmmaker Programs—http://www.nyc.gov/html/film/html/for_residents/star.shtml

Asset, Basis, and Investment Resources

Beneficial Owner Rules—when your parents' names are on the title to your home

- Internal Revenue Regulation 1.163-1—https://www.law.cornell.edu/cfr/text/26/1.163-1

- Journal of Accountancy—http://www.journalofaccountancy.com/issues/2008/oct/equitableownerequals deduction.html

College Application Training—http://collegeapptraining.com

College Application Training TwitterChat with TaxMama—http://collegeapptraining.com/chatcollege-on-tax-tips-and-preparation-for-parents-of-college-bound-students-recap

DirectInvesting.com—formerly the *MoneyPaper*—learn to make tiny investments in corporations with minimal or no fees—https://www.directinvesting.com/index.cfm

How the IRS defines Basis—https://www.irs.gov/taxtopics/tc703.html

HUD-1 Escrow Statement—summary report you get whenever you buy real estate or get a home mortgage loan—http://portal.hud.gov/hudportal/documents/huddoc?id=1.pdf

myRA—mini Roth IRA resource from the US Treasury—
lets you invest in tiny increments, with automatic
withdrawals—https://myra.gov/how-it-works

NetBasis—website designed to help you determine the tax
cost of securities held long-term, and to determine all
the splits and dividend reinvestments over decades of
ownership—www.netbasis.com

OANDA Foreign Currency Resource—http://www.oanda
.com/currency

Saving for College website—http://www.savingforcollege
.com

Tax Theft Loss Tips—TaxMama article—http://www
.marketwatch.com/story/when-might-stock-losses
-count-as-a-theft-claim

Credit Resources

Equifax—http://www.equifax.com/idtheftprotectionkit
(Disclosure: I have been writing a column for them
for several years—http://blog.equifax.com/author/
eva-rosenberg)

Experian—http://www.experian.com/data-breach/
newsletters/child-identity-theft.html

FICO—Fair Isaac Corporation—credit scores—http://www
.fico.com

Trans Union—http://www.transunion.com/childidentitytheft

Money: Generating Cash

AirBnB—rent your home or other real estate—https://www
.airbnb.com

Annual IRS Unclaimed Refund
    announcement—https://www.irs.gov/uac/
    Does-the-IRS-Have-Money-Waiting-For-You%3F
DogVacay—get paid for pet sitting—https://dogvacay.com/
    how-it-works
Lyft—like Uber, get paid for giving people rides—https://
    www.lyft.com
Uber—get paid for giving people rides—https://www.uber
    .com
Unclaimed Money site—https://www.usa.gov/unclaimed
    -money
Wrapify—turn your car into a rolling display ad—http://
    www.wrapify.com/about

Crowdfunding and Gifts

Give Forward—http://www.giveforward.com
GoFundMe—https://www.gofundme.com
TC Memo 2010-286 *Lang v. Commissioner*—winning on the
    issue of taking a medical deduction when someone else
    paid the bills for you—http://www.ustaxcourt.gov/
    InOpHistoric/La5ng.TCM.WPD.pdf
YouCaring—https://www.youcaring.com

Other Useful Reference Materials

About.com—Julie Garber, wills and estate planning expert,
    about the annual gift tax exclusion limits—http://wills
    .about.com/od/understandingestatetaxes/a/historygift
    tax.htm
About.com—Diane Schmidt, moving expert, about
    moving insurance—http://moving.about.com/od/

hiringamovingcompany/tp/Definition-Of-Moving
-Insurance-Terms-You-Should-Know.htm

MarketWatch.com by Dow Jones—http://www.market
watch.com

Small Business and Management website—*the* best place
for clear tables and summaries about tax rates, vehicle
information, depreciation and more—http://www.smbiz
.com

Tax Court Case—*Lori Singleton v. Commissioner,* the nurse
who beat the IRS and deducted her MBA expenses—
http://www.ustaxcourt.gov/InOpHistoric/singleton
-clarke.sum.WPD.pdf

TaxWatch column—http://www.marketwatch.com/topics/
journalists/eva-rosenberg

Politics as Usual

Reach out to your federal legislators and let them know
what you want them to improve or fix—http://taxmama
.com/special-reports/call-to-action

The Tax Policy Center—http://www.taxpolicycenter.org

Some Favorite Resources and Writers

There is no doubt that I will leave people out. There are so many
people whom I admire and respect. They will be added at the
website: www.deducteverythingbook.com

Affiliate Summit—Missy Ward and Shawn Collins took
someone else's failed idea and turned it into a thriving
and profitable resource for all affiliate marketers. Use affiliate marketing to have other people sell your products

and services, only paying them commissions when they actually perform. (Just like Amazon.com does.) The two annual Affiliate Summits are the best place to make contacts and connections and to learn about the tools you need to grow your sales beyond your wildest dreams. They even have a newcomer program to help you get started and to meet the right people—http://www.affiliatesummit.com

American Citizens Abroad—a wealth of tax and other information for Americans living outside the United States—https://americansabroad.org/helpful-information

Amit Chandel, CPA, a.k.a. the TaxGuru—a prolific blogger, tweeter, and Facebook-poster keeping up the latest IRS, CPA, and state news, announcements, and pronouncements with lots of humor. This man keeps me smiling each and every day—https://www.facebook.com/achandel.cpa

Clark Howard—consumer advocate, radio show host, author, entrepreneur, and all-around good guy who looks out for your interests and helps keep you out of trouble—http://www.clarkhoward.com

Deborah Carney—author, photographer, blogger, and a celebration of life in her own right. She's been through a lot and helps others grow and thrive joyfully. Need someone to help promote your books? Talk to Loxly! She'll be your biggest fan—http://bookgoodies.com

Gail Perry, CPA—editor in chief of the *CPA Practice Advisor*, one of 2012's Most Powerful women in Accounting, highly prolific author, instructor, and very patient editor. Gail is another of those people who can make complex concepts simple—like how to develop Excel spreadsheets, macros, and more. She writes books for *Dummies* and *Idiots*, too. Just my speed—http://www.cpapracticeadvisor.com/contact/11272907/gail-perry-cpa

Ilyce Glink—personal finance, real estate, and consumer advice columns, books, and a radio show—http://www .thinkglink.com

Jean Mammen, EA—immersed in international tax knowledge, author and, thankfully, a member of Team TaxMama, answering questions from visa holders, expatriates, and folks with dual residences and lots of things way above TaxMama's head. Her book is well worth reading—http://1040nror1040.com

Jim Blasingame, the small business advocate—award-winning radio host, visionary, writer, and advocate for the rights of all small businessfolks everywhere. Tax-Mama is proud to be a founding member of his brain trust and a regular guest on his daily radio show—http://www.smallbusinessadvocate.com. If you are running a business, you must read his book, *The Age of the Customer* to understand how the market dynamics have changed—and how much more power the customer has than ever before (http://ageofthecustomer .com).

Dr. Judy Rosenberg—Radio personality and founder of the Psychological Healing Center, cousin Judy (yes, I am proud to say she is my first cousin) developed a revolutionary method of therapy through her colorful Mind-Map. Patients coming to her have their issues resolved in only a few sessions, instead of several years—http:// psychologicalhealingcenter.com

Her new book, *Be the Cause: Healing Human Disconnect* was released in time for Thanksgiving 2015 (http:// www.amazon.com/Be-The-Cause-Healing-Disconnect/ dp/1514793032/mywishlistA).

Kathleen Pender—*San Francisco Chronicle* columnist with a financial beat and a Net Worth column. Excellent insights on the latest tax and financial news, breaking

complex concepts down to plain English—http://www
.sfchronicle.com/author/kathleen-pender

Kay Bell—Bankrate editor, writer, and very funny tax blogger, with her finger on the pulse of tax news. With her
background and experience, she knows enough to be a
tax professional, but isn't—http://dontmesswithtaxes
.typepad.com

Kelly Phillips Erb, LLM, JD, and so on, known as the
TaxGirl—tax attorney, author, *Forbes* senior editor and
columnist, and coffee addict with a biting wit—http://
www.taxgirl.com/about-taxgirl

Kris Hix, EA, NTPI Fellow—one of the very first students
at TaxMama's EA course has flourished as a writer,
instructor, and Intuit Tax Answer Expert, as well as an
accomplished tax professional in her own right. These
days she's also an occasional teaching partner with
TaxMama—http://www.northernkentuckytaxservices
.com/index.asp

Larry Lawler, CPA—founder of the American Society of
Tax Problem Solvers. He teaches tax professionals how
to save the lives of taxpayers. He teaches CPAs, EAs,
and attorneys how to negotiate with the IRS to reduce
peoples' tax burdens. Those taxpayers can finally sleep
at night and rebuild their lives—http://www.astps.org/
staff-committees

Liz Weston—author, speaker, and nationally syndicated
personal finance columnist who can make the most
complex money topics understandable to the average
reader—http://asklizweston.com

Melinda Emerson, the Small Biz Lady—a generous, positive force in the universe teaching people to build,
smart, ethical business that succeed. She never fails
to include TaxMama in her annual tax round-up and
TwitterChat—http://succeedasyourownboss.com

Michael Rozbruch, CPA—my teaching buddy at CPE Link and a great inspiration to me. Michael built a multimillion dollar tax resolution practice ethically. His practice even survived a detailed IRS ethics audit—how many people can say that? These days, besides teaching with me, he has built a coaching practice to help other tax professionals market their tax resolution practices. So, like Larry Lawler and Michael, himself, they can save lives too!—http://www.rozstrategies.com

Mike Reed, EA—based in California and our world traveler, joined TaxMama's EA course at the same time as Susan Holtgrefe, EA. Together they created tools, cheat sheets, and spreadsheets to help organize their own studies and shared them with other students. A longtime member of Team TaxMama, Mike can be counted on to clear up confusion in the TaxQuips Forum when it comes to complex issues. Who knows, someday he will be persuaded to teach for us—https://www.linkedin.com/in/mike-reed-687a4232

Pat Lynch—CEO and editor in chief of WomensRadio. com and a variety of related sites to help empower and educate women and men. Along with her husband and daughter, she has built a springboard for men and women to build their careers and to get involved in volunteering—http://www.womensradio.com/author/radiopat/. In fact, she has been hosting all the TaxQuips podcasts for more than a decade—http://taxmama .audioacrobat.com

Rita Lewis, EA—and active member of Team TaxMama, providing answers and guidance in the TaxQuips Forum. She is our go-to person for issues relating to New York and Connecticut taxes, especially for people who work/live across those state lines—http://www .dollarssense.com

Roger B. Adams, EA—based in Portugal, international tax maven, with a very diverse background and a fascinating perspective on tax issues—https://www.irs.gov/Individuals/Acceptance-Agents-Portugal. You will find many of his articles at the American Citizens Abroad website: https://americansabroad.org

Sid Kirchheimer—author and Scam Alert columnist for AARP, a versatile consumer and financial writer who tells it like it is—http://www.aarp.org/money/experts/sid_kirchheimer

Steven J. Fromm—a real Philadelphia lawyer and top tax blogger with powerful insights into estate and tax issues—http://www.sjfpc.com

Susan Holtgrefe, EA—stepped into TaxMama's life as a student and brightened her entire school. This "stay-at-home mom" is never at home because she's busy building a tax practice, volunteering at a VITA site then taking it over as a paid manager, creating tools and resources and study sessions for our students, and teaching in TaxMama's EA course. Meanwhile, she's raising lots of children and their friends with sleepovers, campouts, sports and more—a whirlwind, an inspiration, and a positive force—http://erietaxprep.com/susan-holtgrefe-ea

"Uncle Bill" Porter, EA—Goodness, has it only been three years since Bill graduated from TaxMama's EA course? He's a valuable member of Team TaxMama, often correcting TaxMama herself when she answers too quickly or without looking things up. Uncle Bill keeps TaxMama honest and is a terrific researcher. Based in Minnesota, he's our go-to guy for Midwest and ACA tax issues—http://www.pridetaxpreparation.com

Virginia Lawrence, PhD—creator of award-winning websites, and articles, formats authors' books for the Kindle

(especially Patricia Fry's charming *Klepto-Cat* series).
You met Virginia in Tip #157 where she started vol-
unteering on the Tall Ships well after the age of Social
Security. When I grow up, I want to be like her and Patty
Fry—http://www.cognitext.com

William Perez, EA—tax planning guide at About.com with
lots of reliable, updated resources, and one of TaxMama's first instructors in her online EA Exam School—
http://taxes.about.com

Willie Crawford—one of the kings of the online marketing
kingdom is a man who knows about everything, speaks
a dozen or more languages, has flown hot, military
aircraft, taught martial arts, written a host of books,
ebooks, and cookbooks, has been everywhere—and is
still inspiring new generations to reach new heights.
And he's not even all that old—https://twitter.com/
WillieCrawford

Non-Tax-Related—But Interesting and Fun

Asimov's Three Laws of Robotics—http://www.auburn
.edu/~vestmon/robotics.html

Assistance Dogs International—http://www.assistancedogs
international.org/about-us/types-of-assistance-dogs/
service-dog

Doctors without Borders—http://www.doctorswithout
borders.org

Isaac Asimov—http://www.asimovonline.com/asimov
_home_page.html

Los Angeles Conservancy—https://www.laconservancy.org

Los Angeles Tall Ships—http://www.tallshipsfestivalla.com

Paradise Regained Utila—http://www.paradiseregainedutila
.com

Scientific American—http://www.scientificamerican.com
Vgo Robots—remote presence resources for students and
others—http://www.vgocom.com

TaxMama's Courses That Might Help You

TaxMama's EA Exam Course—become an Enrolled Agent
in about 6 months (it's like a 3-year college course in
taxation, plus an exam review course, all rolled into 6
months)—http://irsexams.com
Live and self-study courses and resources at CPE Link—
http://www.cpelink.com/teamtaxmama. Here are some
you might find useful:
Doing Tax Research Online Using Free Resources—
http://www.cpelink.com/product/detail/?p=6221
&s=85iz6kg
Filing for Innocent Spouse Relief—http://www.cpelink
.com/product/detail/?p=6233&s=85iz6kg
Marijuana's Tax Paradox—http://www.cpelink.com/
product/detail/?p=6219&s=85iz6kg
Mortgage Interest—http://www.cpelink.com/product/
detail/?p=6097&s=85iz6kg
Tax Checklist for Knotty Divorces—http://www.cpelink
.com/product/detail/?p=6181&s=85iz6kg
Ten Steps to Release IRS Levies on Paychecks or Bank
Accounts—http://www.cpelink.com/product/detail/
?p=6197&s=85iz6kg

Index

About TaxMama

The truth is, Eva never, ever, ever wanted to get involved with taxes. EVER!

Taxation is the most complicated area of accounting. The rules change several times a year. Sometimes, they don't change until after the year ends and you wait on pins and needles to learn the rules for *last year's* tax filings. It's like walking on black ice. You never know where the slippery spots are. If you step on one without realizing it, it can be deadly. Besides, there is just so much to learn. All the time.

But somehow, Eva ended up in a national CPA firm's tax department and became fascinated. Having a natural propensity for languages, once Eva realized that she could look upon taxes as a language. It all fell into place for her. The other attraction to this field came with helping people who were in trouble. Eva's problem-solving and trouble-shooting skills helped her see solutions other professionals missed. As a result, she became the go-to person for folks who hadn't filed tax returns for years; people who owed taxes through no fault of their own; people whose lives had devolved into disastrous situations. She even helped one client evolve from (practically) being a depressed, homeless, street person to being a happily married millionaire.

Her passion to help keep people out of trouble led her to set up the TaxMama.com website. It's meant to be a free, safe place to help people like you stay out of tax trouble. TaxMama and her wonderfully generous team answer all questions within about 48 hours. They don't do the computations for people—but they will point you to resources that will help you with your issues. They will provide guidance that might save you hundreds, or even thousands of dollars. They will help you avoid tax penalties—if you ask before you do things. However, in return, you are asked to search the database for answers to questions similar to your situation. Because, yes, there are repetitive questions—and dumb questions.

Another TaxMama passion is to educate tax professionals—in ethics and tax law and procedure. TaxMama was asked to start a school to train tax professionals to pass a rigorous set of Internal Revenue Service licensing examinations—the Special Enrollment Exams (*SEE*). Also known as the Enrolled Agent (or EA) exams. You can find it at www.IRSExams.com. This is the only school of its kind. And it's all online—no driving; no sitting in traffic; no leaving home for a week or a few months. Just log in from your home or office. (Or like one fellow—who logged in from the McDonalds Wi-Fi outside the national park where he spent the summer.) While TaxMama's EA Exam Course includes training and software to help students pass the EA exams, its main purpose is to provide in-depth training on tax laws, tax research, tax practice tools, IRS procedures and taxpayer representation for IRS audits and tax debts. It even trains tax pros how to make a good living. It's like a 3–4 year tax course, all in six months.

Students not only learn how to pass the *SEE*, they are entertained and inspired. The course is a lot of fun—and has been known to change lives—for the better. So if you're looking for a new career . . . if you're feeling like a Tax Nerd (www.TaxNerd.net), join us. Live classes run from May–October or November each year. Self-study classes are open year-round.

Discover Even More Ways to _Save_ Money Every Month!

The Franklin Prosperity Report is dedicated to helping its readers save money each month with creative ways to cut your costs on groceries, insurance, travel, and everyday expenses so you can save more and spend less this year. Named after one of our Founding Fathers, **Benjamin Franklin**, the newsletter follows Franklin's centuries-old wisdom and his principles of building wealth. After all, it was Franklin who said "A Penny Saved Is a Penny Earned," and it is the motto we have adopted for the newsletter.

Each month _The Franklin Prosperity Report_ follows in its namesake's footsteps and gives readers invaluable advice from a host of top-shelf, expert contributors on how to properly manage and maximize your money. Recent issues have included topics such as:

- Cut Your Tax Bill in Retirement! 6 Proven Financial Strategies to Keep More of Your Hard-Earned Cash

- Stop Overpaying for Health Insurance! 8 Ways to Put Your Money to Work for You in a Health Savings Account

- Baby Boomer Guide to a Fully Funded Retirement

If you would like to learn more about joining _The Franklin Prosperity Report_ and how it can help you keep more money in your pocket each month, go to: